SPINE

PRESENCE

J A M E S   L E E

2 0 1 6

SP|NE

THE POST-CONVENTIONAL ZEN TEACHING ON LIFE AND DEATH, GATHER AND LOSS THROUGH MEDITATION AND SEXUAL YOGA

PRESENCE

First edition 2016

ISBN-13: 978-0997697537
ISBN-10: 0997697539

10 9 8 7 6 5 4 3 2

CONTENTS

Chapter 15:

Ending

Giving Love is the Only Salvation 281

Preface:
Zen Is an Empty Page

Preface

Introduction:
The Way of a Book

Truth can't be put into words. An insight is a glimpse of truth. The decomposition of insight makes it less true. But without explanation, an insight may never be seen, just like without partial insights, truth won't be told.

Truth cannot be thought of. The road to truth is paved by the constant understanding of insights. Insights need to be realized on our own, unless it's decomposed into bits and pieces, even though the bits and pieces can never contain either truth or insights.

The magnetic field of earth can be seen as a rough example of truth. To have a glimpse of it, we need a magnet. However, the magnet may never been noticed, unless someone grinds it into a needle, paints one end into red, hangs it by the center, and draws a dial with marked degrees around it. The magnet is you. And that last step, is the book.

This book was written to be a description of insights. It is a signpost following which you are invited to discover. Words can point, and then you have to see it with your own eyes.

The chapters are loosely arranged in progression but not inter-dependent. You are welcome to start from the beginning or jump to any topic. If a concept is too foreign to understand, feel free to skip it.

Life is a practice, and the point of practice is to experience the fundamental truth with your body instead of merely intellect. To know truth is easy, to feel truth is enlightenment, to live truth is the grace of guru.

Our journey starts with the topic of death. With the understanding of death, we are free to explore the dance of life. Eventually, we venture into the domain of relationship and sex, right through the limitations of body and mind.

At the time of editing, it is my wish for us to embrace the flaw of our human-ness, dedicate to living the deepest truth, and let go laughing at the inevitable imperfections.

Now, we begin.

Chapter 1:
Meditation on Life & Death

One Man
Must Die Twice

We can't really enjoy life until we know death. A person who forgets death will try to get something from life, instead of giving himself to life because he knows that he can get nothing in the end. Such a person who can't feel death is full of want and fear, wanting something from life and fearful of losing.

A man has to die before his physical death. Without remembering his pending death, he is drifting in the changing pictures of life.

Human life span is a blink of eye in the history of universe. Remember that you are going to die soon enough, you change the way you produce work, the way you look at women and the way you motivate friends. Not too far from now, your glory and tragedy, your climax and agony will be forgotten without a trace, as if nothing has ever happened.

To die before your physical death is to let go of everything: your identity, your comfort, your security, your ownership and your reassuring arrangements. In the end, we get nothing by clenching for ourselves. Everything will be gone and everyone will leave the party, in days or decades. We are afraid to look at it, and then we realize it too late. Everyone becomes enlightened at the moment of death, as all familiarity becomes a blur, all memories fade. We can't move but surrender open, maybe for the first time of our lives.

If you can let go of all holdings, the openness you become at death will feel like home. Openness is not scary. It is the background behind all manifested forms, inclusive of us. Yet we are often too afraid to rest as it. We occupy our attention with internet, TV, relationships and career, as if they utterly matter. We are scared of sitting alone in an empty room, yet desperately seeking for something to make up stories with. Even a tragic story feels more satisfying than nothing at all. While everything continues to happen –your facebook, your TV, your girlfriend– we are dying. The openness is there and we are denying to feel it.

All fear is the fear of ending, and the fear of ending is the fear of emptiness afterwards. Who are we without a career, a facebook account or a relationship? Spaciousness is the substance of existence, before your physical birth and after your physical death. That spaciousness is who you are that can't be destroyed, as all people and things come and go.

When a crisis happens, we are forced into total surrender. It is the process of death, in that there's nothing you can do to change it. This forced surrender can suddenly make you open just like the white light in your last vision. When all sense of security and personal ownership is taken away, what is left? Whatever is left when you have nothing to cling onto, is who you really are. That openness after the agony of loss is freedom. When you realize that all you have will utterly vanish, your need to acquire loosens. When you realize that all personal ownerships are illusory, there will be nothing you can do but to offer. You no longer work to secure freedom, but to demonstrate freedom. You no longer manipulate to receive sympathy, but stand unapologetically for the sake of love. You learn to feel everyone's suffering just as yours. There's nothing to lose, because you don't have anything to begin with. Your body and mind will betray you. One day your legs are too weak to walk but you still feel like sixteen; one day your mind is distracted even though the person you love dearly is ill. The fate of body and mind is in an unfathomable web of karmic results. No one knows why everything is as it is now. Your physical form grows on its own until it stops one day.

It's a daunting thought thinking about dying. But as a fact, we are ending moment by moment. We just choose to ignore it and then manufacture a continuity through a world of happenings. Just as you read this sentence, the moment has passed. Your relationship with a loved one has just changed a little for better or worse – they make no difference in the end – too little to notice until someone cries out "You changed!" Of course you changed my sweetheart. Change is constant in every fucking thing. Every change is an ending of the old. Every ending is a little death. We are afraid of change because utterly we are all too afraid of dying.

So, why don't you go back to maintain your sense of continuity, absorbed in TV, career, relationships. Until your TV's broken, career's futile, relationships vanish, maybe violently or peacefully. For an instant, the bound to object is forcefully cut. You are exposed wide open. You try to look for security. Where's the ground? Where's the familiarity? As you are in panic, another thing disappears. Whoops, you are in the limbo with no gravity.

Eventually, tension relaxes. Fear turns into humor. *Hey, it's not that bad. Even when I was watching TV absorbed in drama, this limbo was there too.* Limbo is death. Feeling through your daily routine of work and relationship, pleasure and pain, then you know death. Knowing death, your are no longer afraid of change. Money comes and goes, women visit and leave, but the openness of limbo remains. Nothingness is your ultimate fear, but it's also your only constant true nature. Feel the space where everything appears, it's vast and no thing, it contains but doesn't grasp. Happenings are co-arising in this space, agony or sex is just an appearance. It's all a joke that never meant anything. Your heroic romance and inevitable tragedy is no more than a random crack on a wall, until you give it a meaning in order to occupy your attention temporarily.

Death is utter enlightenment. You have nowhere to hide but to be enlightened. All our efforts and devastations are made to postpone various forms of ending. So you eat a burger, build a house, buy some insurance. Enlightenment can be scary. Sometimes a crisis might just be a doorway to go through. Don't turn away from your agony, don't cover up your feeling of lack with ice-cream or niceness. Use your loss as a slide into openness.

You may continue to grow the business, you may continue to nurture relationships. But you know that nothing is ever necessary. Freedom can't be found in any form of acquisition, but is already there as the openness that you try to avoid. Relationship is only a temporary opening to the fundamental love, which is who you are that has no boundary from everything else. Love is openness is death. Are you ready for it?

2.

Skydive
to the Rabbit Hole

Death is being pinned down by enlightenment.
You'd either practice enjoying it while alive, or be
raped to die.

I want to tell you something. Please take a deep breath.
Remember, whatever happens, we love you.

You, could be free falling in the sky, right now.

You got on the plane whose doors were taken out. The
instructor told you to arch your back in the sky and don't
ask why. You have signed the life release form, doomed.

Lifted in the air sitting in a jumpsuit for half an hour,
waiting... You couldn't hear a word but saw people start to
disappear from where the door should be. Pushed to the exit,
arched your back...

You. passed. out.

Yes, right now, you are free falling mid-air. The earth is spinning fast and your face is blown out of shape. I'm glad that you can still hear me in such loud wind...

The question is, would you rather wake up?
If you never wake up, how bad is it?
This is as bad as death ever gets.
But we are having fun here, right?

So here's the old Matrix drill. Blue pill and red pill. In any moment, you always have a choice to embody a deeper truth, or to indulge yourself with however you are taught to live.

C ontrary to the belief that meditation can take you to a state of nice-ness, it, in deed, is done to create the process of death. Spirituality has nothing to do with being happy-and-pleased, but is practiced to stop thoughts.

Total awareness can be a frightening experience, if you are still clenching. Chances are that we all fear the unknown of darkness alone in an empty room. Only very few people have learned to stop mindstream even for seconds.

Who we are is not our body. On a seven-year cycle, every cell of you is replaced. Physical body dies on such a frequency. Yet who you are continues. Quite obviously, you are not your flesh.

Death is the process of consciousness leaving its human form. It's only frightening if you mistake the decaying meat and fluctuating mind as who you are.

Whenever you are ready, try not to think anything, for as long as you can, and then you might feel the pleasure of spacious being-ness right where you are. But this pleasure has nothing similar to that from an ice cream. With space comes the free fall of mind. The free fall of mind is death, pure awareness.

To practice meditation is to actively die, as consciousness is being freed from its bodily residence. You access the depth of existence, regardless of happiness or the lack thereof. When you are afraid of death, meditation will scare the shit out of you.

To meditate is to step into your fear of total nothingness. Our attention tracks motion. As we begin to believe the urgency of the trivial, meditative practice frees attention, bringing you back from appearing events to reality's depth.

Yet the suspension of attention seems threatening. We all say that we want peace. But in effect, we keep creating drama. Peace –though is who you always are and will always be– is frightening to the mind's need to attend motions. As soon as we touch the edge of meditative state, we tend to either phys-ically grab onto something or mentally grasp a thought, which leads to another thought. By attending to happenings, the mind reinforces the idea of me-in-here-experiencing-others-out-there, so that ego can reassure its own existence.

Human body is a vessel, so is human mind. If science is advanced enough, we can manufacture suitable forms to reside in as biological body dies. We can erase memories and reform neurobiological patterns. In such case, your body and mind is like a jacket that can be replaced.

Through meditative practice, we actively abandon body and mind. This in itself is sufficient. In such a state, if action is called upon, one shall act with clarity and efficiency, without fear or hesitation.

3.

Live Consciously
in the Real World

_The Next Step of Spirituality

Enlightenment is not the end, but the beginning.
The art is to express your consciousness through
external forms, so that the world becomes self-
aware. Consciousness recognizes itself as its own
light. We humans are here to unfold this realization.

The question is how much you can be involved in an ambiguous world while maintaining clarity.

Consciousness is the capacity to know and feel. Although it's our nature, we don't always have access to it because we get lost in trivial events. Everything happening, inclusive of your body, your mindstream, your sense of self, your relationship, is constantly in motion. Motion attracts attention. As the result, we are always attending to external happenings.

Traditional spiritual practice involves staying away from the world and its motion. Practitioners sit down for days, weeks or months, facing a blank wall. The world stops. Thinking stops. You are being there as you truly are, the capacity to know and feel, witnessing your own body and mind's tendency to move.

To love is to feel. When you reside in consciousness, you become the pure capacity to witness. Feeling without interpreting, we taste freedom when all motion of mind stops.

Meditation and isolation can sometimes bring you back to consciousness if you are lost in life's events.

Nonetheless, consciousness is who you inevitably are. Its identification is always accessible, whether there's motion or not. If you train yourself not to get lost in events, not to narrow attention, you don't have to be away from the world. In fact, you can stay as the capacity to know and feel even in the most chaotic situations.

You are born as human with body and mind. Mind is a less condensed form of body. Like everything that exists phenomenally, your body and mind is constantly changing. Yes you are the unchanging awareness, but you still show up in a human form. And forms are inherently in motion. By denying desire and fear, you are creating resistance. Although it sometimes keeps you away from human bullshit, this very resistance becomes the source of separation. As a result, the very attempt to be a loving person through meditation becomes the cause of unlove.

Some meditation practitioners carry this resistance towards the outside world. Meanwhile they themselves are suffering in private for their own emotional turmoil. Human crap is always going to be there as long as you remain a human. In a few moments of enlightenment, internal conflicts dissolve. But they tend to come back in the very next second.

The next level of spiritual practice is to co-embrace life and death. Life is your human form, the world's drama, as well as the chaos in your head. Death is the all-aware *nothingness*. Consciousness doesn't have motion because it is *no thing*. It feels and knows, while doesn't have a self. It is like a mirror that reflects all, yet not having a quality. Either events are happening or not, thoughts are moving or not, consciousness is always behind what's appearing.

Advanced training is to access consciousness in the midst of an emotion or a desire. Instead of suppressing your human nature, you feel it thoroughly, while maintaining the witness position, not hiding, not grasping.

Meditation can bring you back to consciousness from your own thoughts. But if you believe that thoughts and emotions are inherently bad, you tend to create separation which is iron-ically at odds with the inclusive nature of consciousness. You then are denying your own form, through which consciousness supposed to come.

If you are a tree, you won't have thoughts, but you will have leaves, roots and veins. For a tree, leaves, roots and veins are the form that consciousness come through. As human, mind and body are your non-negatable residence, even though they are unnecessary and annoying.

As humans, let's take a look at our own experience.

In every moment there are two aspects that are happening: appearance and the perceiver of appearance. The perceiver of appearance is consciousness, while the appearance is always trying to distract it from being conscious. Think of it as sex: a man has to be undistractably conscious to be a trustable lover, but the feminine beauty will indulge with everything to distract his awareness. In life, we are often absorbed in our own stories and thoughts, forgetting that we are consciousness that can't die or even be affected. The art starts as you live the little story of success and failure, romance and rejection, yet always remembering that you are the boundless capacity to feel. Nothing more.

This is the true practice. Knowing death, yet not afraid of life. Living life, yet always feel death. Unless your nature as consciousness realizes itself already dead, the possibility of ending will always feel like a threat.

We are habitually attending to events in order to gain a sense of existence. Relationship spoils neediness. Careers reinforce identity. We tense up our body to construct a muscular shell for security, while anxiously patching up a pity self-image. We are unable to sit in a room of nothing. And now, our sense of pride is disturbed by these words.

Next time when you feel trapped by life's drama, try not to resist your less-conscious friends, relational commitments or taking roles in this world. But always remember that you will die one day. Every one will leave everyone of us. You will lose everything that you ever own. All securities we create are going to fall. What's left is the capacity to watch and know. This is who you are in essence, either orgasming in an orgy or injured in a car accident.

This practice of remembering death while living life soon evolves into an art of knowing how much to be in the world. Your capacity to remain consciousness in motion will develop over time, but no matter how good of a practitioner you are, there is always a point where you get caught up in events. Like in any type of training, you grow by leaning over your edge, by participating in the world a little bit more than you are comfortable with. But as soon as you find your consciousness wavering, come back before you step out again.

There, meditation is the most effective way to come back to consciousness through, whenever you realize that you have got lost in the appearing happenings. Motion is not something to feel to, but to feel *through*. When you can't feel through, reduce motion temporarily to meditate in formal period of pure witnessing.

Like a sailor on the sea. A good sailor is not afraid of big waves. However, no matter how good of a sailor you are, there is always a big wave that can knock you down. Your capacity to handle waves will develop. But if you can't handle it for now, come back before you sail out again.

Chapter 2:
Expand Awareness

4.

Attention...........

_Meditation is the Suspension

*You can't meditate by trying to do it. Meditation
only happens, never being done.*

Meditation happens effortlessly. All practices should
be felt and done out of spontaneity. To recognize
consciousness is not to add force, but to relax as
the spacious freedom of size-less self. By nature you are consciousness already. You just need to rest into it.

Panoramic awareness is the suspension of attention. By
suspending it from being narrowed, you free tension. Whatever task you have to perform throughout the day, you can do
so with non-reduced awareness. Widen it, suspend it, and let
attention expand voluntarily.

Fear and want can't exist without you giving attention. Consciousness is space. In this space, there is energy that is spontaneously directed to form appearances. The director is causality. Causation is a function of space. Light energy is being caused to crystallize into forms, and instantly released from forms. All light is the light of consciousness, and consciousness is the space for light to be. They are not two, but only two aspects of the one. When you loosen attention's knot, consciousness is no longer folding onto its appearing self as if there's an other. Empty space is the only substance. It is the canvas for painting and stage for dancing. Attention only forms when consciousness folds onto itself. The complexity of folding is our drama.

When you undo the folding, you are free from karma. In a deeper perspective, nothing is significant enough to deserve a narrowed leaning-forward. The cause of every appearance is consciousness itself. Only when we forget – or never realize – that all happenings are the appearance of consciousness, are we interested in them as if there is an other to attend to. When you mistake what you see to be something out there to put attention onto, you create a knot, and another knot. This leads to a complex mess which we call life. In truth, your life is never as solid as you believe. Whether it's your children's smile or your girlfriend's jumping-up-and-down-like-a-kid-on-the-mattress-of-new-home, everything of life is already loosened and gone as you realize it. The nanosecond time lag between the actual event and your brain's comprehension, inevitably caused by the speed limitation of light and neurotransmission, guarantees that whatever you think as now has already been in the past.

Meditation is to loosen the grip of your attention – the focal point of suspended awareness. Consciousness is felt when your attention is expanded as awareness. This awareness gets narrowed every time you grasp onto thoughts, experiences, objects or persons. Attention is the knotted awareness. Whenever attention is freed like the last entanglement untied, relaxation and alertness come after.

Sex and finance are the biggest distractions around which we wrap our adult attention, and in which hope and fear come together. Things were either better or worse in the past, as they will get either better or worse in the future. You want it to be better, you are afraid it to get worse. Awareness becomes focalized onto the fear of failure.

As we hope to escape from life's constraints, true freedom comes when you let go of all hope. You may never find anyone to understand you. In fact, you will be more misunderstood as your developmental level exceeds world's comprehension. When that happens, the need for approval has to simultaneously evolve into compassion for ignorance, in yourself and others. This is not to be confused with egoistic superiority, but is similar to the love you have for your children, in that you unquestionably accept their developmental limits. You probably didn't expect the child to understand your opinion on the political situations in the Mid East, as you took into account of the preference for mushroom veggie soup for her barbie dolls.

Nothing of importance is ever gained or lost. Everything is still appearing as you hit or miss. It's all wide open undone. We think freedom and love can only be found when something pending is brought to completion. Yet freedom and love is already the nature of this place. It's something to be realized and then expressed, not something to be found. It is what shows in your surroundings right now, as well as what showed in your dream last night. It appears spontaneously as it disappears simultaneously, in a dream or right now.

While you magnify the potential of self and the world, live the journey already arrived. The freedom we can ever find is here as always, though we tend to forget and then chase one thing after another. When you look for freedom and love on the outside, you can be free and loving right here. All you need is the assertiveness to let go of attention's grip.

5.

The Birth of a Slut

ttention tracks motion. To track motion, the mind has to recognize objects through the seeing of shapes. There are two ways to free your attention:

- One is to dis-identify with shapes.
- The other is to be ok with the unknown result of change.

Tension is created whenever we are unwilling to let go of the desire to know where everything goes. We usually forget that all results of change that are seemingly in time are actually rising in space as a web. Expecting anything in time is a futile effort.

The dissolution of concepts starts with the dis-identification of shapes. In order to make sense of the world, we name objects, a tree, a bird, a snail. And then to make sense of our human life, we give names to associations and experiences, a friend, a wife, a colleague, an enemy, or, a date, a fight, a fallout, a one-night stand. We seem to have mapped out a lot of happenings and roles within the happenings. But in the process of naming, we isolate parts from the whole. Once we isolate, the mind starts tracking. This naming and then attending to change is extremely satisfying to the mind. In fact, this is the only way the mind can comprehend reality.

The problem is that the reality of existence is too vast and intertwined to be precisely labeled by names. The mind draws a grid with concepts, and then try to fit everything into this grid. As change happens in an isolated object, our attention tracks the change and attempts to put it in another concepts. The relational concepts of stranger turning into friend turning into girlfriend turning into wife turning into plaintiff is a result of this naming and change-tracking game of the mind.

A bird lands on the tree as a gust blows the leaves.

This makes sense. But it is not what actually happened. The more encompassing truth is that the tree is a mutant part of earth that grows upward, the bird is a tip of the tree that can depart, the air is a layer of the bird with less density. Yet this is still not the ultimate truth. What actually happened is that there's nothing to be called a tree a bird or a gust. It is an entire current of multidimensional vision that just moved internally as a whole.

This is the ultimate truth of all changes in nature, career, and relationships – the entire current of multidimensional vibration that has moved as a whole. It is the answer to your sex and divorce, lottery and bankruptcy.

But it doesn't satisfy the mind's need to know. The mind needs labels – tree, bird, gust, as well as landing and blowing to describe the sense perception of truth. It has to reduce it to pieces and chunks. It suck shit.

Our entire drama of struggle is out of this trivial description of visions. To be free from life story's dissatisfaction is to be disillusioned with this reduction of truth.

We can do it in two steps:

- First, see and perceive without naming. Once you give it a name, it becomes a concept. And your relationship to the actuality has been shifted to a mental concept.
- When you see a situation or view, do not isolate shapes, and do not identify objects based on the shapes that you tend to recognize. See everything as colors and black-gray-white values of shade. All that you can perceive with eyes are just colors and dark-to-light values. That is it.

When you are in relating with another human. Don't give the situation a name, don't make a *relate* into a *ship*. Every time you label a thing, you are illuded by the pre-assumption and past experience of this label. Every human relationship with anyone in any moment is unique and will never be repeated again. When you label it, you miss the nuance. The relating-ship is changing shape constantly, but the concept of a label is static.

The ship will incrementally shift without you aware of it, until it changes so apparently that your previous conceptual label can't match the reality anymore. When you label someone as a girlfriend, most of us have already disconnected with that person as she is, but only as a role in your repertoire of concepts. You change every day, she changes every day, how you relate changes every time you are in contact. In stead of being tuned to the moment-by-moment reality, you keep the concept of the girlfriend and see her as this concept. It's funny that when sometimes you have been with someone for long enough and you call each other honey. One day you realize that even calling that person by name feels alienated. She has completely become your preconceptualized role of honey. A year goes by, you look at her and seems she still fits the role. Until one day your honey spills in someone else's bedroom. You get mad but your anger has nothing to do with love or relating with the person. It is out of the breakage of concept. Who is getting mad? It's your mind. What does a mind want? To put dynamic happenings into static grid. What happens if something doesn't fit in your grid of comprehension? Your mind gets irritated. Now your honey is on someone else's dick, which means that this person doesn't fit in the concept of honey anymore. The mind still refuses to relate directly with what's happening, but keeps looking for new roles for reality to fit in. The mind searches for the repertoire of names...Slut! Ha, found it! You are a slut! It all makes sense again. You are a slut on a dick! Now the mind is satisfied.

Our human drama usually has nothing to do with love or reality. It's a role play illusion where sometimes you get a horse with a horn, and it's not quite a unicorn because it also has a pig tail. You can try to invent new names like upigorn, yet only end up it turning into a fish. Now ufishorn starts to sound French.

Ridiculous as this process is, we are doing it constantly. We label realities such as heterosexual, homosexual, monogamous, polygamous, polyamorous, homomonopolyamorous... It just doesn't end, yet nothing can ever capture what actually is happening in your closet – a temporary multidimensional formation of the entirety of vibration in dead-silence space.

Whenever you name a thing, you are setting yourself up for disappointment. The incremental changing process will one day transform every drop of honey into a slut. The reality is in motion. Concept is dead and stiff. It can't contain the dynamics of uniqueness of each moment.

And so, here are the ways out of this homomonopolyamorous insanity:

- Do not identify a shape as an object.
- Do not name any happenings.
- Let go.
- Let go of the need for stability.
- Let go of the curiosity to know where it goes.

Everything is in motion with unknowable amount of nuances. Relate with what is. But only right now.

6.

Here Comes
the Urge to Pee

*Attending to events strengthens ego's need to know
that it exists. Ego's constant want and fear is the
source of resistance, which creates all suffering.*

Any thought or event you attend to becomes a focal
point of infinite consciousness.

The world is in flux. There are always endless happenings that demand your attention. You can easily be caught in the events, not realizing the totality of life that rises altogether.

There's nothing wrong with attending to events. Working, eating, peeing, scratching. Events happen as long as you remain human. However, human form is only your appearance. The awareness of this fact is who you truly are. A computer that can talk to you doesn't know who she is, but you do. That awareness is you, even if you wake up one day with a body of a laptop. Bodies are machines. It works until it doesn't, all of which doesn't make a difference to who you are.

Anytime we lock our attention onto anything, or even form an attention at all, we begin to forget who we are as wide open awareness, and yet mistake a series of remembered past, imagined future and interpreted story as who we are.

So why do we attend to anything anyway?

We go to work, eat healthy, answer texts, clean the house, because we want to make better of our lives. Even the choice of going to a toilet is out of the unwillingness to be filthy wearing wet pants.

However, only a separated self has a life of preference. By attending to happenings, you are wanting to make your life better and yet fearing it getting worse. This fear-and-want further renders the outline of separation, which leads to alienation and deep-rooted loneliness.

Now seeing that the will to go to the bathroom is just ego's need for comfort and self acceptance. Do you bother to respond your urge to pee at all? Do you attend life events at all?

First of all, you shouldn't close down to experiencing any happenings in life. This closure is also building the walls of separation. It is ok to participate in events, as long as you are in for the fun of it. You go to the toilet for the humor of our human domain of experience. And occasionally also let go to enjoy the fun of not responding to this urge.

Ultimately you do not have a concrete life solidified with stories. Only your separated self has a story. And that separation is the source of un-loving.

Attention is locked onto anything only when consciousness forgets that everything is contained in itself. It sees itself as someone else to be dealt with. When you free your attention, you free the world. The world is only your appearance rising in space.

Next time when you can't stop thoughts, try to widen your attention. Thoughts, like everything else, can't exist without your participation. If you don't attend to your thought, it dissolves. Your memories, you fearful thinking, they can't persist without you attending to it. Conversely, the more you react to happenings, the more complex the drama evolves. Your attention is feeding whatever is happening with more complexity.

If you can undo consciousness's first folding onto itself, which is the formation of attention, your grip will relax open, alert as space instead of a focalized point. Awareness opens outside-in without being channeled into attention.

Chapter 3:
Step into Duality

A Universal Love Story

Ladies and gentleman, let's play it cute with a romance story:

A long... long time ago, the sky and earth were blended, there was no distinction of things but all a blur. There wasn't up or down, inside or outside. Of this size-less blend, lives Prince Conscious and Princess Light. One day, with a loud thunder, the blend was torn apart. For the first time, a gap showed up and Princess Light was taken away, trapped in a cage, frozen into matter, locked in another realm. Consciousness can no longer see Light.

The Prince starts to look for Light. He manifests materials, liquids, and then incarnate as replicable organisms in the realm where Light was taken. Those entities evolve over time. They discovered a less condensed world above.

The Prince's incarnation continues to evolve. They grow the ability to reflex, in order to adapt the changing terrains of jungle, mountain, desert. They create settlements and transportations. They have lived for billions of years through body replication. Each new born replicant has been ingrained with the mission to search for meaning.

A long time has past, they are sometimes distracted. But the sense of mission never stop striking the chord in their innermost mechanism. The incarnation has spread into millions of individual forms in a place where they are awed by the beauty of frozen Light. She has been here. But where is she? Every time they see the trace of Light, their hearts open, they want to know for absolute.

Consciousness has loved Light for eons. He stands in front of a trace of Light and remembered beyond this realm. He felt the answer. In the beating of heart, the same non-separated knowing. She is here. Seeing through the imprisonment he knows her for who she truly is even though she can't remember herself.

In an instant, they both realize, that this entire realm of the manifested, itself and everything it contains, is the Light of Consciousness. For eons of searching, they have never left one another.

The end.

Now you may act upon vomiting.

Truth is the union between consciousness and light. They are one at first. And then being pulled apart into two aspects, one as consciousness, the other as light. Without conscious space, light has no where to be. Without light's movement, conscious nothing-ness can't be defined through contrast. They can't exist without each other.

They appear in the same place every day, but can't see the other. They both feel a deep rooted lack, the yearning for someone to make whole with. Day after day, year after year, consciousness and light seek one another. Little do they know that they have never been apart since the birth of universe. They always have each other, but are lost in the search. They hardly realized that the other is right where they are.

As humans, there are two approaches to feel truth – through consciousness identification and light identification. You can only know truth by being it. Consciousness and light are two qualities of the same *one*.

To be truth:
- Option one is to realize *conscious-light*, the self lit-up consciousness that remembers itself.
- Option two is to reside as the *cognizant* aspect of this conscious-light.
- Option three is to dance as love's *light*.

The practice of feeling this ultimate truth often involves either *witnessing* or *dancing* with energy. In other words, you access your true nature, as well as the nature of all existence by *seeing light* or by *being seen as light*.

Ultimately, consciousness is light, freedom is love. But the approach to freedom and to love varies hugely. When you are perfectly conscious, you're also love, because these two are never apart. You can't be conscious and hateful at once. When you are completely love, you become suddenly conscious of everything, including the fact that you are love.

There are practices that require you to be consciousness and love simultaneously to start with, such as stand-up comedy and certain styles of music performance. In such cases, you are performing as light, but at the same time draw back as consciousness to play your own speech, body and mind as undisturbed witness.

Good comedians are perfect examples. Humor necessitates one to stand outside of a situation to make comment on it. When you draw yourself outside of a situation, looking at it as if it's all a massive joke, you are consciousness, who knows light perfectly, as a joke in this case. However, consciousness itself is a deep silence, it knows and feels without participating, or talking. This is why traditional spiritual trainings are all about sitting in silence.

To say anything or to perform a comedy show, you have to illuminate. Comedians have to move around, talk shit, radiating some sort of light. And what's behind this light? The perfect undisturbed consciousness that sees everything as a cosmic JOKE. Comedies often bring audience love's openness. Why? Because love is the union of consciousness and light. It is the playground of humor. Humor is to access the spacious consciousness and put it in light's performance, so that it reminds people of the inseparable nature of two aspects of love, sometimes in a shocking unexpected fashion.

Other than some comprehensive practices as both consciousness and light, there are one-sided approaches: to be the witness, or to be the witnessed. The destination is the same, only means vary.

We often think of spiritual practice as the perfect peace of meditation. We assume that to be enlightened, you have to sit down in front of a wall or stare at a candle, shit like that. Because all texts on human spirit describe it as the correct way. Buddha sat for decades, Jesus walked the desert, Gandhi was abstinent, Eckhart Tolle paused for half a minute in an audio book letting everyone wonder either the book's over or he fell off a chair. All those people, wrote shit down.

Writing shit down requires concentration and renunciation. There are a thousand pleasurable things you can otherwise do as you are writing. You could have being shopping, sexing, traveling, singing, but you choose the singularity among all possibilities. On the other hand, light is energy. It's all over the place. It's explosive and powerful, but has zero structure. Consciousness is emptiness. It has no content, no quality in itself. Without happenings of itself, consciousness is free from possibilities. Therefore, it is capable of directionality and structure. It is capable of reducing all possibilities into one decision – writing shit down.

Whoever likes to write shit down, he is inherently on the route of consciousness.

This leaves the spiritual approach of light undocumented, unstructured, unanalyzed. Only a few have realized that you can access the feeling of love, the essence of all beings even through ice-cream and shopping, if done properly. You can dance your way to God. But you won't be documenting your way to God while dancing it. Those who write it down are balding old men who sit still on the meditation pillows.

Here is what's happening for many people who seem inclined to meditate. Our current culture relates value to getting shit done. Therefore, consciousness and its outcome is regarded as more valuable than the capacity to move energy, which is light. These cultures shift, but this is where we're at currently. All humans have full access to consciousness and luminance. But each individual has an essence within the scale of the two extremes. If you naturally prefer shopping, dancing, eating sweet, conversation, you have a luminance essence. If you are inclined to hunting, climbing rocks, observing, accomplishing goals, or anything requires focus, you have a conscious essence. This essence can shift in one person over time, but is not a choice. Anything you choose to be is a shell covering over the true self. You are most satisfied and feeling-right when you are living according to your true sexual essence. This essence is not gender defined though most males have a conscious essence and most females have a luminance essence. Some people have an essence right in the middle.

The practice is to trust your true essence, and go all the way with it without adding any personal preference. Consciousness-inclined humans can go for activities that require concentration, while luminance-inclined humans may go all the way with the flowing movement of energy.

If a woman with luminance essence distrusts the power of her own inclination, fear will obstruct natural growth. She may take on the masculine methods, such as rigid meditation attempts or forceful career climbing. She will be physically tightened as she resists her desire to be seen as light's radiance. She might cultivate a successful career, but still not feeling a life that is happy and fulfilled.

David Deida is a teacher on spirituality in sexuality. He addresses the different spiritual approaches for masculine people and feminine people better than anyone. As I realize that whatever I say on this subject is going to parrot his words, I'll share the wisdom:

Consciousness is about nothing, and light is about everything. A masculine person believes that nothing matters because all people die and all arrangements loosen. Everything is no more than a temporary display that's subject to change. And if it is not permanent, it doesn't worth my attention. So the masculine consciousness is always trying to feel deeper than appearance. And the empty spaciousness is the only thing that never changes. It was there before the Big Bang, and will be here after the universe. Therefore I should probably put my attention on this eternal emptiness.

However, light is not about the orientation of attention. It is the flow of energy. Everything that appears is energy, and therefore everything matters. The ear ring matters, the dress matters, the shape of a fork on dinner table matters... The man across the table finds her extremely cute and refreshing when she gets exited about the silver finish of a fork, but he knows that he, she, whatever fork, are all going to be utterly forgotten. Life is cute, but insignificant.

To feel truth is to take your essence to the extreme. If you want the freedom of emptiness, don't just masturbate and feel the temporary release of tension. Take it all the way to recognize the empty nature of this moment. How long does an appearance last? Look back at everything that you've gotten, they are all gone. So is this moment as you finish reading.

If you want ice-cream and beautiful textures of furniture. Take it all the way. Yes everything matters. But feel it all happens at the same time, instead of one after another. Smell of the ocean, sound of the leaves, shape of cloud, texture of the wood floor, temperature of the sun, animals in the jungle, stories in time past-and-future, they are all co-arising as a whole. You can be the appearance without trying to draw back, all appearances at the same time. This is the proper practice of luminance in the Feminine approach.

When you take your essence's practice all the way, you realize that through emptiness you also feel everything, and through fullness you also see the empty background beyond. In fact, emptiness and fullness are the same word. When a container is full of water, it's also empty to a fish. In the end, emptiness is fullness, freedom is love, consciousness is light. They take opposite directions, and yet arrive in unity with the other. This is the ONE truth of all experiences and the wisdom for all actions.

8.

Self Love?

The sense of "me" is a stress that comes after fear.
The placement of "other" is the discrimination for
what's not "me".

L ove is to be one with. Self love is the dissolution of
boundary.

The separation between you and yourself is also the
separation between you and the world. You will always feel
alone in the context of gaining and losing. A divided entity can
accumulate or disintegrate, while the whole remains neither
aggrandized or reduced. When you love yourself with intensity,
your acceptance of world's appearance is unconditional. Success
no longer needs to be celebrated and rejection won't be noticed.
That non-judgment is the dissolution of ego. Unconditional
offering is the end of separation.

The feeling of alienation dissolves when you cease holding a conceptualized image as self. There will be no longer an other, but all a blended field. The feeling of blurring-together becomes your primary experience. Seeing through the external obstructions, you no longer regard yourself as a separated thing in a world that is out there.

The practice is then expanded to serve others. When you master the art of seeing the essence regardless of appearing stories, you are capable of becoming one with everyone regardless of their shapes.

Some people have misunderstood love as something to be found. It's an illusory mission. Love is the very fundamental of all existence. It is the union between the container and the content. You are reading this book in this moment. Take a second and look around where you are, maybe a room with walls and a desk, maybe in public with people walking around. No matter where the appearing environments are, the fundamental of perception consists of three aspects, a background, a perceiver, and a perceived. Who you are that is experiencing the room is the watcher, while the room is the content. Laying in a bed reading, you assume that *you* are in this room. Yet the deeper truth is that *you* don't have a place to be, and *you* don't have a size. *You* can't be any-specific-where. Yet this place appears in *you*. You are always outside of this room. Look around. Can you feel the slightest feeling that you are outside of all this?

Look back at everything in the room. You are also all this. You are also the *room*. The feeling of both inside the room and outside the room is the union between the perceiver and the appearance, the union between the size-less container and the shining-sticky content. This is not a visualization, but a realization. It can be realized as a fundamental here-ness. This here-ness is always happening as long as any form of experience is taking place. This union between the *you* that is always outside of this room and the *you* that is the room, is the only truth that's beyond time, the only love that can't be mended. And this love is not to be found in anywhere. People and events can serve as a reminder of this deeper love. But whether the reminder presents or not, you have to realize proactively. Not to visualize, because once you start to imagine, it becomes a mental concept, a philosophy that represents truth, but is not truth.

Now that we realized what love is. It is not to be found in experiences or companionships, but to be felt in all conditions.

We are humans, which are a part of the whole. We are like cells, as there are good cells and bad cells. We don't want to be a cancer cell. But every time when we transmit closure to the atmosphere, we are being a cancer cell. The art of being a good cell is to remind other cells of this fundamental love that is already every cell. To this point, love is not just a truth, but also an act. It is like martial arts that you have to practice every day. And a lot of those trainings may seem trivial, non-practical, waste-of-time. Wax on wax off, you never know how much power you cultivate through the waste-of-time practices until the practical moment comes. Love is something that you do.

You are a reminder armed with the clear trust of truth, so that this trust of love opens everybody's heart.

Meditation, chanting, and reading scriptures are the traditional ways. Singing, contemplating, dancing, taking a martial art class, learning Hatha Yoga, going to an art show or a musical, are the modern ways. It's true that the practice of love can be expanded in our time.

In the end, no matter what the approaches are, we probably still can't find lasting love in this world. But we can choose to feel and transmit love. When you express the deepest truth, then you see. You see that there is never a lack. Love is abundant and you can remind others of this truth in your own way.

9.

The Universe in a Ping-Pong Ball

Duality is the source for all complexity and conflicts. Yet it is also the source for all dynamic and polarity.

The phenomenal world exists in polarity, in duality. Cold vs. hot, birth vs. death, above vs. below, like vs. hate, one cannot exist without the other. A person never suffered won't know happiness. A person never faced death won't know life. The external world, which consists of materials, concepts, ideas, sensations, exists only because there's polarity between two opposites.

Yet behind this tension, there's eternity, that has no opposite. It is of the is-ness of is. You can call that thing consciousness, emptiness, nothing, love, God. But to not confuse, we call it the *oneness* for now.

Here's something strange:

Before the birth of the universe, it was the size of a Ping-Pong ball. What is the size of a ball? —*Nothing*. Literally, *nothing* is a size of a ball. We can't even discuss where it is because the space as we know doesn't exist yet. It is a limbo, and a ball. Whatever you call that ball, it is of *one*. Then it exploded in a sudden. During the expansion, matters are born. Because objects are now floating, there also come distances between objects. That distances among separated material objects, is called space. Therefore space was born as definable. Materials and the space in between are in constant change. Therefore time is implied, conceptually existing with reference of human memories and projections.

The phenomenal world was born in the Big Bang. Whatever it has become, that oneness of Ping-Pong ball has been separated, trapped in material objects.

It's still *one*, but separated in the external existence. Whenever our identification is on the external level, we experience separation, and consequently, duality. And there you have struggles and suffering, or so called unhappiness.

To be happy is an instant endeavor, that is to identify with the eternal oneness of all things, being present. It is an instant realization, but not a permanent one. All spiritual practice is done to come back to this realization over and over.

Happiness is more than deep throat or chocolate cake. Sensory pleasures are caused by stimulations recognized through external identification, which also happens to be the context of duality and unhappiness. If chocolate makes you happy, a lack of tasty food will make you unhappy. They share the same source. Real happiness is always here fundamentally. It is the default state of being. Everything can potentially blind you from it, but nothing can alter it.

Concepts and thoughts only exist in the phenomenal world. Here is an Easter-egg secret. If you can look around without any naming or even forming a word, you will instantly feel absolutely happy regardless of the situation. Just by perceiving without labeling or thinking.

We experience this in front of nature's wonder. Facing a massive waterfall in the jungle, we are awed to have no thought in mind. There comes a gap between thoughts. This is when expansion occurs. This is when you are being present and cool.

With practice, you can maintain this thoughtless state for longer period of time. Once you are capable of doing so, spontaneity is made space for, as a primal intelligence. All great arts, discoveries, realizations inevitably happen in this space. If you maintain present without thoughts, you will feel at ease all the time.

And now... What? Thought you might ask.

A table doesn't have thought either. Yes you can just be, but a rock can just be as well. As consciousness in human form, shouldn't I be creating a better self to embody this realization?

To the next chapter.

Chapter 4:
Create
a Better Self

10.

The Paradox of Self

True confidence comes from the non-existence of ego. We have a self that is pure perception, that never grasp or run. But we also have a superficial self that lives in gain and loss. The possibility and memory of gaining and losing give us fear and greed. We want something, and at the same time are afraid of losing something. This superficial self blinds us from our true self. In moments of openness, maybe when embracing a lover, contemplating a nature, maybe when facing death or the possibility of so, our true self comes out of shells. It shines for moments, but eventually becomes covered up again by selfishness.

Self-development may involve skill learning and physical perfection. These are not always necessarily to be denied, but the ultimate achievement is to be the fearless self that sees humor in all drama yet not being a member of it. It expresses and manifests without holding back. It fucks everything open.

When we are attempting to improve ourselves, which is a virtuous effort, we are inherently trying to gain something, a better self perhaps. This possibility of gaining implies its opposite – losing. You then see gain and loss for the future, and may very likely be comparing with those in the past. You want to be better, but afraid of getting worse. There, greed and fear perpetuate. To say greed may be a bit condescending. After all, the greed is towards a perfect self that helps others and the world in consequence. But even a good will can put you in a state of constant wanting, which leads you to self-ishness in full circle.

When you are wanting to get or fearing to lose, you can't possibly be your true self. To a point, self-development becomes a shell of self-identity trying to break itself. Problem is, ego can never kill itself. Any effort to do so will only strengthen it. The more you want to dis-identify with an illusion, the more you are assuming that there is an illusion. That is how an illusion perpetuates.

Once again, let's take a look at the true self that we are talking about in the following exercise:

Every moment of experience contains two components – a perceiver, and a perceived. Right now, you can notice what you see – shapes and colors. Notice sounds – the exhaust of a car on the street, the wind through the window, or your own breath in a quiet room. In this process of perception, there is something noticed, visually and auditorily. Yet there is also something that is noticing the colors and sounds. Who is perceiving? That which is noticing its own experience, is who you are beyond life's changing frames.

When you have a thought in your mind. You can choose to go after that thought or let it pass without attending to it. The capacity that notices your thoughts is the same capacity that perceives colors and sounds. That ultimate end-perceiver that is witnessing everything happening, yet doesn't have a quality of its own, is the one you call you. That is the one that was there ten years ago, is here now, and will be here a decade later. Your body has grown up, your mind patterns have been reformed, yet who you are stays exactly silent and still.

When you are embracing your lover, when you are contemplating wonder, all worries fade, you are left to be who you are without shell. The same you that was here from as early as you can remember. In moments of fearlessness and having-nothing-to-lose, you are for real. That is the one with ultimate power. And that power can use your human form to create.

The challenge is that we can hardly sustain that having-nothing-to-lose state. There are always something seemingly important and urgent. Why do we attend anything to begin with? To move away from loss and towards gain. This losing and gaining doesn't have to be of material, but also of self-image or status in the crowd, or even the virtuous progress of self-development for the sake of serving others. All those moving away or towards, strengthens a sense of self with want and fear. This false self is what we identify with most of our lives.

11.

The Power of Nobody

The ego in oneself needs security and comfort. The masculine side of it searches for power to secure freedom, not knowing that the wall of security encloses his own prison.

Fearlessness has nothing to do with acting macho. Virtue doesn't require a good person to come through. All concepts of macho and good person are images of superficiality. Just like in any other pursuits, you will always feel not macho enough or not good enough. Self-development is an endless abysmal that can never get you the absolute perfection of freedom.

The basis of self-development is the existence of a solid me that inhabits in a human body that is separated from the outside world. And we are now strategizing to make supreme of this solid me. As long as there is a concept of me at all, it's always subject to change, for the superior or inferior. Fear and want follow.

To be absolutely free from fear and want, to have untamed power, is to evaporate the concept of self. Instead of looking at yourself thinking you are going to make yourself stronger and more beneficent, be who you are. Not who you are as a bundle of described qualities. But who you are that is free from the need for qualities, the one that was there always, silent and unchanging, that does one thing and one thing only – perceive. It is aware of everything yet not grasping for fear of change, or running away in face of chaos. It is the pure perceptive capacity that can't be attacked or lost. It is complete on its own and doesn't need anything.

We are constantly looking for something to complete our lives – a house, a career, a nice car, a relationship. Have you ever gotten anything that you thought would ultimately complete you? Remember when you were a kid that you believe if you get that toy car then every problem of your life will be insignificant forever, or when you were pursuing a girl in high school and believed that if only you get this girl in your life you will never want anything more? How long did the satisfaction last? Did the toy car solve your problems for how long? Did you still feel the sense of lack a few years into the relationship? LOL. Even now, do you still believe that if one day something happens, graduation, promotion, career, marriage with a sweetheart, kids growing up, gaining health, or anything at all will solve your fundamental sense of lack? In that case, you are a dog chasing its own tail. No one will ever get there and stay for long. Every arrangement that you can ever acquire, will only satisfy a momentary need, and then you will want something else to complete your life or to free you from life.

Most people spend their entire life chasing their own ass on a hamster wheel. They believe that life will be better once something happens. Some of them actually are skilled and disciplined enough to make their goals come true. They might have moments of satisfaction, while some of them don't even have. It's just another moment, no different from this one or any one moment. They have gone a long way, but the sense of fundamental lack and the need to acquire never lessen.

Telling anyone to let go is like an offense. Even telling ourselves to let to. *Let go of that career that you never liked. Let go of that girl in the past.* Then the superficial self that you think you are speaks:

How could you even say this to yourself? Remember how you worked hard in school for this career? Remember those nights you share personal secrets with this girl?

Here is life. The moment you realize it happens, it's already gone. And it will be like this forever. Until you stop chasing anything, and realize that this moment, is as good as any moment is ever going to get. If only you can realize it.

Everything that can happen, is something that can be noticed. If it can be noticed, it has a quality. If it has a quality, it is appearing. To have an experience with any appearance at all, there must be a perceiver. This perceiver is consciousness. It feels everything, every emotion and motion, yet doesn't have movement or emotion of its own. This consciousness is not bound or trapped in your skull. It is who you were, are and will be. Take a second to look around where you are. Consciousness is not *in* here, but *here* rises in consciousness. Who you truly are is *where* this place appears. It is perfectly complete because it doesn't have a quality or quantity of its own.

The world can't be without consciousness. But consciousness does not need an appearing world to stay *nothing*, and certainly doesn't need the appearing condition to be a certain way. Whenever you are attached to anything, it is the superficial self that sees potential loss. Consciousness has nothing to lose. It is empty. It can't get better or worse even though its content will. Consciousness is the only perfection that there is. Because it's impossible to get better, it doesn't want. Because it's impossible to get worse, it doesn't fear. Everything you try to achieve through self-improvement, you are, already.

If you want freedom, you are that already. This is why you are attracted to be free to begin with. But as we mistake a solid existence to be ourselves, we try to get freedom with this assumed solid human mental-emotional-physical form, not knowing that the very assumption of this solidity is the reason that we are not free. Instead of chasing freedom with a separated human body, why not just be the consciousness within which all drama occurs? Whenever you are totally conscious, you can't possibly feel trapped or take happenings personal. There's no persons or traps, everything happens is like a dream that is rising in consciousness. The dreamer is free, even though he might assume his dream identity to be solid.

The practice then, shifts from getting somewhere to going *through* right here. Freedom and love is right here. Unconstrained and effortless. If only you can stop clenching and tightening. Clenching and tightening are out of insecurity of total nothingness, mentally, emotionally and physically. To be enlightened, you do not need to go seek. All you need is to realize. The practice is still necessary, but it is no longer to get you somewhere else. True practice is always to realize a deeper truth of existence, right where you are, right through the changing moods and circumstances. Good training is always to be the true self that doesn't have a self-image or quality of any kind. It is like an eye that can't judge itself, but sees everything else.

12.

The Posture of Now

B reath is the portal between internal and external. It can only be full in an upright posture.

Posture is a response to your sense of security. Your mind is always looking to understand where you are and what's going on. When you are not sure if you are safe, you create tension in order to feel that you are in control, muscularly and emotionally. However, if you trust the unknown nature of this very moment, your mind and body can then relax. Where you psychologically think you are and what is going on on the surface don't matter that much anymore. It's always the same openness that contains all that's happening.

Trust is essential. Knowing that nothing matters is essential. Your posture will respond into a correct position when you feel secure for the trust of openness.

Occasionally, mind takes over and creates fear. That fear tenses up your body. There are two approaches to dissolve fear and correct posture:

- One is to stop mind's interference, by being consciousness.
- The other is to take some parts of the shell of protective closure, and break it with the body.

Breath and posture are the tangible ones to correct. Once you deliberately release the tension in breath and posture, the hardened shell is broken. Your body and mind can relax for you to settle as openness.

Breath and posture collapse and emotional collapse are always packaged together. Therefore, by correcting some part of the habit such as posture, you break the entire structure of fear. That's why whenever people lift their chest, a suddenly feeling of courage rises as a result. The shell from insecurity is broken as you embody trust through your posture and breathing.

Supposedly, good habits should be landed spontaneously. When you are present, at ease, aware why you are alive, your posture will adjust itself in a mighty shape. The problem comes as mind and body develop their shells and kinks. When we are acting through habits of closure, which is out of touch with who you truly are, which tends to forget why you are alive in this moment, our breath and posture collapse. This is when deliberate correction becomes necessary.

Posture correction is effectively used to heal emotional contortions. Your physical kink is a reflection of your emotional kink. When emotional disposition is right on, your posture should be perfectly right. When the emotional self is fluid, posture and breathing will respond to it. However, since every body goes through shit, it's useful to utilize deliberate correction of posture to slide out of mind's pattern of recoil.

Can being present fix posture?

Being present can only help with posture if the person is unkinked, which is hardly anyone. For a person who has emotional or physical kinks, being present won't fix his posture or breathing much. Think of Steven Hawking. The state of his presence or the lack thereof won't affect his posture as much. In a way, our mind and body are all wounded more or less. The scar obstructs our presence from coming out through our posture. This is when therapy comes necessary, and is why proactive correction is helpful.

For a perfectly physically and emotionally healthy functionable person who has acquired skills of proper walking and standing, being present can fix his posture instantly. Consciousness can come through a healthy body and mind, in techniques of walking and standing, without obstruction.

13.

Skill Development vs. Enlightenment

_Awareness in the Middle of Motion

B y nature, we are evolved to develop the correct way of breathing and standing like other animals do. But because of the interference from mind, we grow false habits based on fear and the tension of hope. Eventually we were abused as kids, rejected as adults. We retract our chest and shorten our breath, tensing up to protect ourselves from being hurt. That's how we fuck up our natural posture and breathing. Taking over the natural way, bad habits of movement create closure in us and people around, even though we want to be open and relate with other humans – most of whose bodies are fearfully shut down as much as ours. What practice involves is to utilize mind purposefully to counteract bad habits and develop new postures that transmits consciousness. Over time, these new habits become natural, so that your body can rest into them intuitively, so that you can be present as consciousness, no longer need mind's discipline.

What Is Skill Development?

To live as a gift is to express consciousness through human form with developed skills. However, enlightenment and skill practice hardly coexist. Skill practice includes internal training, external training and acquiring techniques. Internal practice is to regulate breath and internal energy with mind, as external practice is to gain muscle and flexibility as well as to maintain physical health. The technique aspect is languaging and action, similar to playing sports or instruments. How to stand and sit – or play piano or practice martial arts – in a way that transmits consciousness and love, what words to use to evoke openness in other people, are in the domain of skills.

What Is Enlightenment?

All skill trainings – internal or external or technical – are in the realm of manifestation. They are the art of expressing consciousness. But you have to have consciousness first. Otherwise, we are just pretentious posers. Consciousness is accessed whenever you are disillusioned with body and mind, as well as the solidity of the surrounding world. Enlightenment is being consciousness. When you are in a dream, you might suddenly become aware that you are dreaming, but the dream continues. This is the feeling of conscious space. Enlightenment is the disillusion of mind, in a dream or awake.

How to Become Enlightened? What Interferes in Awareness?
As much as what to say and do matter, words and deeds often utilize our mind. Whenever you think about what to say next, you can't maintain the meditative awareness. You then get caught up on the fluctuation of thinking. Enlightenment is to be consciousness, which is your nature but you tend to ignore. We usually mistake mind and body as who we are. The feeling of enlightenment is being present and aware. The practice to settle in this state is meditation, which is to stop mind, and therefore realize consciousness – the sudden feeling of *"Oh, there I am."*

The reason that we are not conscious all the time is that our mind habitually streams. Want and fear, strategizing, remembering and imagining. We are attending to our thoughts from awaking to sleeping. When you stop thoughts through meditative practice – which could take form in walking in the forest or playing basketball or sitting in front of a wall – you become the witnessing all-pervasive nothing, watching the tendency of rising thoughts together with appearing existence, without need to grasp.

The Conflict Between Enlightenment and Skill Practice:
The problem comes when you need to correct a breathing pattern or a posture. You have to utilize mind to correct a bad habit, and then to hold the correct posture in place. Once mind is activated, it goes on streaming. We are habitually attending to thoughts, and therefore we lose presence.

The whole point of developing skill such as breathing and posture is to express consciousness through human flesh. Now because you are caught up in the correction, you lose touch with consciousness. We usually see enlightened people walking around with horrible posture or speech patterns. In whatever moment you are enlightened, you don't care about standing straight. The essential feeling of enlightenment is that everything is perfectly fine the way they are, nothing needs to be done or avoid. That is also why enlightened beings often have limited influence to the world, in comparison to the unenlightened ones. They become enlightened without the skill – or motive– to transmit their truth to other humans, potentially through art, posture, breathing, projects. Of course, once you are enlightened, you don't really care about influencing the world any more than your own posture.

How to Develop Skills While Stay Enlightened?
For the sake of enlightenment, recognizing consciousness and stabilizing that recognition is enough. But to be enlightened in form of human flesh that eats and shits and sexes and dies. Skills become important in enlightenment as a human form, not a cloud, not a tree.

Once a new habit of breathing or posturing is developed, you don't need to think. Before that, maintaining consciousness while making correction with your mind is difficult. It requires you to use mind with no digression. You are thinking to some degree but not drowning yourself with thoughts. Mind becomes a sharpened tool instead of a sense of self. *"Breathe deeper"*, *"Lift your chest"*, *"Relax your shoulder"*, your mind is at work. At the same time, maintain the deep blissful feeling of spaciousness. You are the space where all bodies and minds happen, whether you hunch your shoulder or not, whether your mind stops or not. As useful as meditation, the next level of spiritual practice is to meditate in the midst of thoughts. Your mind is thinking, but your attention is open as space. Whether you are telling yourself to lift up chest a little more, or writing a business plan, in the midst of that, you can be aware that everything is just an appearance as if in a dream, already gone as you perceive.

Posture correction or any correction of habit takes mind to direct. It is easier to be meditating as consciousness when mind is stopped. However, consciousness is who you are whether you are thinking or not. Spiritual practice is to feel this, without thoughts, or in the middle of thoughts.

14.

Be Still
and Yet Able to Act

The difference between meditation and deep dreamless sleep is the readiness of mind and body. In both dreamless sleep and meditation, your mind is empty and body is still. But in meditation, the mind is capable to reflex with clarity and focus, as the body is ready to sprint with agility and force.

Some lizards in the desert can stay absolutely motionless for hours. But when they are to strike, they can be faster than human eye's tracking. After the attack, the lizard returns motionless again, as if nothing has happened.

To move around doesn't mean you have plenty of energy, but just means that you are leaking energy. Staying still is just nothing if unable to act. Be able to stay absolutely still, and yet be ready to act with clarity and no hesitation in any necessary moment is the advanced practice.

15.

Retrain
Your Nervous System

*Practice should be done in a formal block of time,
and let go of throughout the day.*

When you are correctly doing anything described in this book, you won't be thinking of it. On the contrary, when you are commenting on yourself, you are no longer participating. I used to play soccer. But I don't watch. If I have to watch on TV, I turn off the audio. The commentators are entertainers. The reality they talk about has nothing to do with what is experienced in the field. A soccer player often runs excessively, feeling the burning in his chest and lung while inhale. His legs are sore but alive. He sees that a teammate has got the ball and he is in the position from which they can pull off an attack... A commentator would miss the experiential nuances, but only see what appears to happen.

Any practice at all is to be done as a training session over and over again so that it becomes a reflex of your nervous system. When situation presents, your body and mind complex will act spontaneously as you have been trained to. This takes time and persistence. Wax on wax off, art is not a short cut, but a cultivation.

You sure can use some of the techniques on spot and see the effect it has with immediacy. If you imagine that you are surrounded by water and you are moving in water that ripples outward, your movement will be more graceful. But if imagining water is all you do, you are just thinking of water rather than being present. Any effort will make you mechanic, even those that are meant to help you gain fluidity.

The proper long-term cultivation is to design a set of practice, meditation, feeling-space-as-water, chanting or singing, contemplating, as a formal session daily. And persist in practicing without commentating. Every once in a while, you reflect and refine the training. But most of time you do it without expecting results. If all you are obsessed with is to meditate, you won't be able to do it, but merely think of it. Some people who are foreign to those trainings will say that a practitioner is obsessed with meditation. Yet this is paradoxically impossible. Meditation and other similar trainings are here to get rid of obsession. Nobody wants to do it, or not want to do it. Practitioners just have to sit down and be still for no reason. It's a spontaneous need. A martial artist stands with bent legs for hours a day. It's not fun, or not fun. It's simply a doing.

Besides the daily practice, you should let go of the training in real life situations. Merge into any situation that you are in without prescription. It should be a direct relationship with people and surroundings rather than a conceptual one. Any concept you hold will make you rigid and quite inhuman. Occasionally, it might be helpful to do practice on spot for just a second in order to come back to awareness in your daily round. You might find yourself visualizing water rippling outward as you move through space prior to meeting a lover, or close your eyes to see dot on the meditation wall before offering guidance to a person in need. However, this in-the-field application should not be an escape from the situation, but rather to help feeling the situation in a more personally-merged reality.

Trivial practice is to be done every day. Over months or even only weeks, your nervous system is going to change. And then your body and mind patterns will be upgraded, and your reflex to matters will be organic and effortless. The old habits are still there, but you can act through the new ones in stead. Meditation, yoga, internal martial arts, painting, music, those are perfect subjects to participate for a clean and heartful system.

Chapter 5:
Embrace the Imperfect Self

16.

The Way of the Broken Man

Art is further stretching, pushing the edge, shining the bright light through a dysfunctional human.

If what you need is healing, creating art will cause further injury. Happiness usually means a rush of abundant energy flowing through a body and mind without obstruction. As we grow older, it's quite impossible not to get wounded by life. Every time you feel hurt, your heart cringes. Physically, you hunch your shoulders to protect the chest area. This contraction brings about a layer of shell. Then people act without authenticity. Their heart is still alive, but covered up. Occasionally, maybe awed by nature, kissed by lover, reminded by childbirth, or reset by death, the light of their heart shines through the shell. But it quickly becomes covered again.

Only a few choose to keep their hearts exposed in all conditions. They insist acting from the heart in front of all threats. We love them. But their heart is wounded by our mistrust and abandonment. Their heart is tender but crushed by disappointment. In fact, this is the path of warrior, to remain vulnerable in front of other's closure. If this is what you choose, you have to face your own therapeutic marks. It's not a shameful thing to deal with at all. Weak people close down and run away when going gets tough, courage is to remain open in face of discomfort.

"If necessary, a man should live with a hurting heart rather than a closed one." Someone else said this.[1] It is an useful reminder when you want to dig a hole in the ground to bury your head like an ostrich.

The question is: what do you do with a hurt heart?

As a man grows older, he might realize that personal happiness is no longer a priority. Happiness is often quite shallow and short-lived. He might still do yoga or sing opera to make himself fluid. But it's not for himself anymore. He knows that others are more likely to receive his help if it's packaged with a bright energy. Sometimes his happiness alone can open other's heart, even more so than practical support. Happiness itself becomes a crucifixion. Such a person may soon realize the lasting joyful-ness that comes with peace. When all the dancing crap subsides, the basis of being is the lasting subject

---

1   David Deida, *The Way of the Superior Man*, 2004

of contemplation. Now happiness has a new meaning. And it becomes significant again.

This concludes the whole story of happiness.

What else is here for people who are injured along the way? How do you live with a hurt heart and keep it open?

If a block of wood has a whirl on it, it might make a beautiful piece of furniture, but not a structural column. When light is expressed through a twisted glass, it becomes artwork projected on the wall. All arts are twisted. If you ever pay attention to the pop romance songs, it won't take long to realize how dysfunctional and therapeutically unhealthy the lyrics are. Love songs are the bible of human neediness and fear of loss. Though there are humorous ones, most Rap songs are butt-hurt explosions of chronic constipation. But we love those twisted songs. Otherwise all that we listen to would be Ave Maria. And if we really want to examine it, even Ave Maria is twisted. Emotional mind is often molded into weird shapes after a few romantic relationships, if it survived your parents' influence first. Good news is that no matter how twisted your mind patterns have become, you can shine light trough a dysfunctional form, Van Gogh, Picasso, rock stars. People love them because there's light coming out of their art. And it's not a bright pure light that is high up there, but a beaten-up fucked-up chalk-board-scratching struggling light down here. The more emotionally crazy they are, the more articulated their arts become, as long as they can keep the torch shining behind the whirl.

This is a dangerous game to live as art. Living as pure light is high up there and risk free. But to be art is to vulnerably express a crushed or permanently drugged heart. Their body-mind complex is heading towards self destruction as many great artist were suicidal. And because the ways they kill themselves are so authentic and tender, their death becomes part of their art. They eventually remained a open heart till it's ground into dust.

So here are three potential endings for those who choose to remain heart open:

1. You get wounded to destruction.
2. At some point you start to recoil. You realize that you have given too much and have to close the door now, because you have given up hope on the world.
3. You keep the door open, but when the world hurts you to a dangerous degree, you stop offering and heal temporarily. And then, you open up the door again.

In the third option, you become a flame that offers heat to the wind. Closing down to rekindle if necessary, once grown big, you keep giving warmth.

There's no other way to live than to give warmth to the wind that is going to swallow you alive in the end. Any other way is coping and suffering. Some people blame the wind and build a blocking shield. Their life remained shallow and unsatisfied. Others die in the burst of giving. They lived without holding back, but their giving wasn't to its potential because they haven't stayed long enough to. It is art, we cry over their tragedy and honor their death.

There are some with both heart and wisdom, who undertake the third option. They offer vulnerly to the world. Along the way they get a few wounds. They keep the trust and proactively open up when the heart wants to recoil. They expose their soul to be squeezed into dysfunctional shapes, and keep shining light through these shapes. From time to time, it comes to the point of close-down-or-die. They make wise decisions to withdraw from wind and therapize their dysfunctions. When the heart is healed just enough to open and feel again, they get out to the world giving from what's left, knowing that a total therapeutic recovery may never be possible. Good enough is art. Staying in the sanctuary is a waste of hope.

All the while they might begin to see the humor of the whole thing. They begin to see the joy of the big picture. Open offering and private therapy, it's all insignificant and deeply joyful.

This is the superior way of giving and conservation, out of bravery and wisdom.

17.

The Origin
of Abandonment

The opposite of self love is not necessarily self hatred, but self abandonment. When we were kids, we identify ourselves with our parents. Every time they didn't give attention, we feel abandoned. Growing up means to dis-identify with external conditions. Therefore it is always some forms of leaving home. Be it physical shelter, financial stability, relational arrangements or emotional ease. As we grow older, our identification of home shifts from parents to a partner. This partner serves as your security just like your parents did when you were an infant. When this person leaves you, you feel absolutely abandoned. This shocking feeling of lack is not only caused by the partner, but is originated way back in the child-hood experiences of being ignored by parents. The neurological pattern of helplessness formed when your mother pretended not hearing you crying thirty years ago is now being triggered.

Infants cry to get attention, this is an evolutionary mechanism that has helped our species survive back in the prehistorical tribe where an infant was left unattended in the woods. A loud cry often gets more attention than a silent grief. Crying is a response of being hurt. It was this hurt that evoked females to pick up such helpless infants, whom we become descendants of.

In our time, or any time, no one can do a parenting job perfectly. No matter how evolved human beings your parents are, there are always moments of misjudgment or overlook that cause the child to feel abandoned. When a lover leaves you thirty years later, this pattern replays. The abandonment issue that has been in dormant for decades now explodes in you as an adult.

We humans have a tendency to fill up emptiness. So that whenever alone, we start to run movies in the head. Often times, the movie is a past experience, a programed belief, a habitual feeling or an imaginary event. Although life is usually neutral, what we tend to remember the most are the negative moments. Therefore the sad romance movie is replayed every day, unobservedly. If you really get a notebook to archive all events in a year, it's likely that the moments when you were cared for and the moments when you were betrayed are roughly in equal amount. But we tend to grab onto the negative experiences as if it is an immediate threat that needs to be redirected. This attentiveness to negative events reassures our abandonment mark.

The bad news is that once a pattern is there, it may never be completely removed. It is remembered like your first language, which you can pick up in days even after decades of not speaking.

The good news is that you can learn new languages and stop using the old. Emotional habits are learned. They can be replaced by healthy ones, as long as you are disillusioned enough to be willing to.

Whenever you play the sad movie, you repeat the old emotional language. To learn the new, a good practice is to revisit the scene with new emotions.

Here's what you can do:
• First, become aware of your own breathing, feeling the energetic field of the body from hands to feet. Put attention on the aliveness of every cell of your body.
• Now, maintaining the awareness of this moment, revisit the scene where you felt alone and abandoned. But this time you are there to support that kid. Knowing what you know now, you are there to send strength to the individual that you used to call you.

All things drift apart, from leaves in pond to continents of earth. Because of the inherited survival mechanism of crying infants, we experience the departure of others as abandonment towards us. When you replay the old programs, you are actively creating abandonment over again. People will leave, things will fall. Even a relationship that supported you to get over loss will come to its own end. As long as you are still here, you shouldn't abandon yourself. This is the one step you have to take on your own. Emotions are addictive, and you might not want to change it. In front of you is only a blind leap of faith.

18.

Do You Need Therapy?

Time eventually heals, if you don't cause further injury. Identification with body and mind often leads to strengthening the sense of self. This self prefers a injured self than no self. This self keeps causing injury based on a reconstructed past and an imagined future to make up a victim. It rather be a victim than nothing at all. You are injured further more by this need for victim identity.

If enlightenment happens, self can disappear. You become no thing, not grabbing onto any identity, winner or victim. You then stop feeding the wound. You then allow time to heal you.

Enlightenment is a sudden rising from suffering. Therefore misery can be a catalyst for enlightenment. But if you cling onto misery to be enlightened because of habit, it becomes an addiction. Like all drugs, the need for misery will further injure you. Then the very misery that motivates you towards depth is also an obstacle to enlightenment, as it feeds the ego. Grievance itself becomes part of ego's identity. And the more identification with external happenings, the more hindrance in accessing depth.

So should we deal with therapeutic dysfunctions at all?
Emotional problems are psychological. It's a mind pattern that is in – the mind. By making it a problem to deal with, you unintentionally utilize mind to affirm its existence. Therapy can work. But identification with it can, on the other hand, feed it. Dealing with therapeutic dysfunctions either makes the problem less by to-the-point treatment, or makes it persist by assuming that the problem exist. The problem is in your mind's continuity. If you assume it is there, it is there. If you can do therapy willingly without knowing you have a therapeutic problem, you can then heal without further stretching the wound. But why would you go to do therapy without knowing you got a problem? Every time you do therapy, there are two opposing forces – *healing* and *identifying* with the dysfunction. One fixes you, while the other keeps you wounded.

Time eventually heals. It's possible that you will carry some therapeutic issues for life, if your biological life span is not long enough to allow time to heal you. It often happens. Then it's a discussion about accepting your limits and being who you truly are in spite of the limits. Therapeutically speaking, the safe and immediate approach is to stop identifying with the dysfunctions. On the one hand you stop feeding it, while on the other hand you expand your attention beyond problems. The expansion of attention is enlightenment. Enlightenment is sufficient. Therefore, ignoring your therapeutic issue has an immediate contribution spiritually, as well as offer a long-term sanctuary space for natural healing.

Is this an avoidance of psychological problem? Yes. But between avoiding the problem allowing it to be solved by itself, and keeping scratching the wound making it worse, choose one.

Of course ego wants to grab onto something. To the ego, even a dysfunctional persisting pattern is better than nothing at all. How to stop the ego? By stopping identification, with therapeutic problems first.

Chapter 6:
Intelligence Beyond the Mind

19.

The Development of Mind Intelligence

I n a life time, the capacity of our mind doesn't increase much. The mind capacity of the brightest individual is not necessarily bigger than that of an average teenager with fully developed brain. What make one "intelligent" are the skills developed over experiences and the ability to eliminate distractions from the mind itself. By recognizing the witnessing aspect in you, you are free of mind's obstruction, so that mind can work spontaneously without hindrance from agenda.

To be capable in intelligence is to gain skills and experiences, as well as to be free from distractions. Skill learning takes a lifetime with no end. The ability of focus is the ability of conscious witnessing. Witnessing happens in the moment, with no graduality in time. The awareness for undisturbed witnessing is what exponentially increases mind's efficiency. And then training over time will stabilize this state of clarity.

20.

The Evolution of Spine

You are both in this human domain and outside of it.
Spine is the interface between the two realms.

I n my own practice, I have been trying to balance between skill development and meditation. To be consciousness is to realize that nothing matters, including your posture. Awareness by itself doesn't have a form. But we are here as humans, which can express consciousness in the domain of forms. A tree or a stone or a sea turtle would live as consciousness through their experiences different than ours.

As human we are inherently involved in the extras. It seems like that we have two choices. One is to abandon body, the other is to utilize body. Ramana Maharshi or Gandhi might be regarded as the examples of abandoning bodily condition for the sake of pristine awareness.

However, profound recognition won't ultimately get us out of the human realm. You still need to pee. And peeing is an action that is unnecessary to consciousness. So you get out of the chair, walk to the bathroom, unzip your pants, pull out your junk, and release your bladder tension. This whole series of action can be done artfully or discordantly. No matter how evolved of consciousness you are, the klutzy digging of penis with a hunched shoulder and a out-sticking head is disturbing to the person standing at the next urinal. Your artless movement might just closed his heart and grossed him out a little, he might pee in his pants a little because he wants to get out of there fast. Now your attempt to magnifying consciousness by abandoning bodily artfulness has just rippled out an unconscious pee-in-the-pants-a-little. He walked out of the restroom self-criticizing and anxious if female colleagues see the wet spot on his crutch. Or if he is like me, he purposefully splash more water on his pants so it looks like water from the sink instead of bladder. Now he went back to a meeting afraid to stand up, so he passed the presentation opportunity. The supposedly beneficent project proposal wasn't accepted. Now your practice of being present, helping the world has just expressed the opposite.

If only you have stood up with structural dignity, walked to the urinal with grace, pulled out your penis like a warrior showing his sword, released your bladder tension like a meteor across the sky, the guy next to you might open his heart more because of your fluid presence.

It is a choice. You can be present in the moment and pee in a hundred positions. Some are less disturbing to look at than others. As consciousness that has taken residence in human form, you can ignore it or practice how to wipe out penis like a package of delicate art.

Imagine a spiritual Guru that smells bad. Hair comes out of his nose, white accumulates on the corner of his mouth, spits fly to the audience and occasionally a huge drool falling from his lower lip... He speaks the words of truth that can light up your dark past, can heal your wound, can inspire your soul. But you find yourself hard to not be distracted by the clumsy way of expression, even though he speaks the words of openness.

We have the choice to just be consciousness, or also be the embodiment of consciousness that reminds others of truth without even talking. That is a beautiful art to practice. People have been practicing chanting, singing, dancing, Parkour, Yoga, Tai Chi, structural integration, Alexander Techniques to develop this skill.

However, we encounter a problem here. Meditation at core is about not giving a fuck. It trains you to realize that nothing is that big of a deal. It is an instant realization. The misconception is that through meditative practice, maybe in a cave or in a monastery, maybe adapting a religion or burning incense to a statue, you can get to another stage of being that is permanently clear. This seems what practice is about, like climbing a hierarchical ladder. However, the truth is that enlightenment exists without the movement of time. You can be completely selfless and loving in a few moments, but turn into a heartless bastard the next day. The practice is not to get you anywhere higher – that is where day dreaming and mental masturbation takes you. Instead, it brings you back to the bodily feeling of loving and selflessness again and again without slipping into the bastard mode.

On the other hand, skill practice is a cultivation. It takes time, reflection of result, and error correction. In other words, you have to take it pretty seriously to develop skill in anything. Think of playing piano or painting or martial arts. It's every day of error correction and micro management. Even the most graceful way to wipe out a penis that gives everyone a chill through spine, can take years to master.

To give a fuck, or not to give a fuck. That's our lever.

In meditation, you realize that nothing is needed. The skill of art requires you to look at a mirror and give a damn on every single little detail. How you breathe, how you stand, how relaxed your shoulders and eyes and neck are, whether your mouth is open or closed, tongue resting on the roof or bottom, whether you use just two fingers to clip the penis or to grab it with your palm. Anything you do in any moment is rippling out an effect internally and externally that can cause a series of events.

When you are practicing meditation and the outward expression of consciousness, you may find yourself in constant conflicts. Whenever I stand straight, bend my knees slightly, relax pelvis, push out my chest, breathe as deep as I can, lower my chin, I can't be in that peace that has been achieved through meditation. Whenever I regain clear awareness by sitting in front of a wall for hours, my chest is hunched and my head is forward. I couldn't seem to care about both.

I know that there must be something that I can orient my attention to, so that my body aligns instantaneously, while consciousness stays unwavering. If consciousness is coming through our human form, there must be a major residence of consciousness in the body that is manifesting the position and movement of the rest of body. As long as I can find it and feel it, the attention to it will both embody awareness and adjust posture.

Here are pieces of my discovery:

• Wing Chun is a martial art style that emphasizes centerline. The entire philosophy is to guard a virtualized vertical line in the bodily center and to attack that of the opponent. The combat is about pushing everything out to the side and fight for the control in the center. It is a martial art that brings people to the clarity of efficient movement.

• When I meditate, I find out a residing feeling on the back of head right above the neck. Whenever I'm aware and alert, the feeling is that my awareness has moved and condensed from the face to the side of head and eventually gathered in the back of head and neck. If I bring the attention downward, I can eventually feel a vertical line in the backside of my body from head to neck even to the tailbone. It is the feeling of centerline in martial arts, but it is slightly towards the back. That feeling of backward is a feeling of witnessing. The masculine people loves observation. When we go hunting in the forest, the feeling is that "I am in here, looking at what's out there." You are still and disappeared under camouflage, while remaining extremely sensitive to any movement from near to far. This feeling of witnessing comes alive when I feel the vertical centerline through the back side of my body. Whether facing a wall of walking or driving, that alertness is the same. It's a disposition of laying back with no content of itself, and witness appearance in the surroundings.

• In evolution, a major milestone was the development of spine. We originated as boneless soft creatures in the ocean, to animals that can walk on land. Once we have a spine, we can stand up. Why are tall people considered sexy? Why is the billboard of a romantic comedy often showing a man lovingly looking down at a happy woman who's head rotates up as they shorten proximity, instead of the other way around?

The secret of consciousness and its embodiment, is in the spine. Our spine is the direct residence of consciousness. It is the control center of the body goes from the bodily base all the way up to the brain. It has its own reflex mechanism that functions without your mind. When you accidentally touch something hot, your hands retrieve back before your mind realizes it's hot. When a doctor hits your knee with a little hammer, your leg jumps upward without you thinking. It is the central of your bodily existence. When you were in your mother's womb, the spine was the first thing developed. Once you have a spine, you have come to this world.

Animals that have developed spines are more intelligent than the rest. It is a sign of advancement. When a man facing down towards a woman as they approach closer, there are two things happening. By lowering down his chin and rotate his head forward, the neck part of his spine is elongated, as the spaces between bones increase. If the woman trusts this man emotionally, she would unintentionally lift up her chin and look up at him. This movement compresses her spine to be shorter. As the man and the woman come closer in this way, his spine becomes longer while hers becomes shorter. This is an unnoticed act of her surrendering herself as a love jellyfish to his structure.

Posture is something important for a man, as consciousness needs a place to park. Intuitively, a well-developed spine represents a man's maturity level in evolution. In polarity between man and woman, the masculine partner is responsible for the structure – where do we go to eat, how do we lay out a plan for the summer. The feminine partner is responsible for energy. Only when the spine of a man is well developed – in both literal and metaphorical ways – can a woman let go of her own structure and trust his direction. She can let go of her angularity that maybe necessary at work, come home and melt into sweet jelly all over his man, as long as the man has an elongated spin, literally and metaphorically.

We always come back to the question of who we are. Of course, we are consciousness, but that is not all that there is. There are also plenty of forms. If you can read these words, chances are the form you reside in is a human. Where do you exactly reside in and through this body then? What defined you as some-body? If a person is missing his arm or leg, it doesn't affect our comprehension of who he is. But if someone's spine is taken out for some reason... Just feel it. Merely thinking of taking out a spine can give you a chalk-board-scratching sound.

There are something in your physical body that can't gain or lose anything. It is free-standing. You might gain weight or lose weight. Therefore, if you identify yourself as meat, you can diminish. But if you feel yourself as spine, you are always you. The entire perceptual ability of human is in the spinal chord up to the brain. The spine and brain can be seen as two independent nervous systems, but for now, let's consider them an integrated piece. It perceives what your sense organs touch, and makes commands on its own. When we talk about primordial intelligence, spontaneity is the automatic reflex from your spinal chord. Everything comes from the spinal chord is always faster with more clarity than that from the brain. Brain adds too much complexity because its memory mechanism is more subject to reformation than that of the nervous system in spine. You can certainly reprogram spine intelligence – nervous system – through your life habits, but it more or less stays recognizable and universal. Yet brains are reprogrammed very differently from individual to individual. They are usually full of shit. To act spontaneously means to act with the direct reflective command made by spine intelligence, instead of going through mind's complication.

Imagine that we do not have this spine intelligence but only live by analyzed decisions from the mind:

You accidentally put your left hand into a fire. You didn't notice in the first half second. Then you turn your head and see a hand on fire.

"Is it my hand?" You think.

Your sight traces back through your arms, *"Um, it is my hand."*

"Wow, my hand is on fire." "This is kind of cool, remember when I was a kid my dad used to teach us how to make fire with sparks from a stone. I never really lit up the flame. But my sister did. She thought she's smarter than me. I hated her for a while. Haha, but it doesn't matter now. She's getting married next week and I'm so happy for her. Remember when we were young..." All the while, your hand is still in the fire. *"Ah! My hand starts to hurt. No, it's not hurt, it's burnt. Or should I say burning. Shut up. Do something about it! Alright, just think. Wait a minute, I can actually contract my bicep to lift up the forearm. Oh no, look at those biceps. I have to start going to the gym tomorrow..."*

This is what we are doing whole day for our lives – trying to make decisions with mind. It's insane but because we all do it, nobody has realized how dumb it is to live in your head. With the reflex of central nerves, the instant you touch the hot fire, before the bioelectric signals even reach the brain, your spine has already made a clear command to jump your hand out of fire. That is the intelligence of intuition that we can trust for everyday life.

Spine is what perceives. It is the embodiment of consciousness. It doesn't have a self that's full of meat, can't be affected because it has nothing to lose or gain. It stands free amidst of all appearances, in spite of emotions that happen in the frontal body of belly and chest. Whenever you can really feel who you are at your spine from upper-back neck down. You can elongate it by rotating your head up and forward, lifting up the spaces in between bone sections. Consciously articulate spine's curvature, and then you are both correcting posture and feeling the feeler. This is the practice of both *being* and *expressing* awareness.

When you are singing or talking, instead of habitually tensing up your neck in the front, feel that what makes sound is the spinal chord at the backside of your neck. You deliberately loosen up your mouth, lower jaw and neck muscle. Speak, as if the energy carried by breath modulation is generated from and going through the space in the spinal backside of head and neck just below the skull.

Eventually you can articulate your expression of presence by feeling different sections of the spine. The study of chakra system in Yoga and the spine channel in Qigong are also references that can add qualities to your embodiment of presence.

21.

Consciousness in a Tingling Spine

_Spine as the Interface Between Consciousness and the Manifested World

S pine is the only part of body that is not affected by emotions. Emotions and body are interconnected. When you have an emotional breakdown, it shows in your body as a hunched shoulder, sunken chest, shallow breath, tightened neck and jaw. If emotional stagnation persists for too long, it brings out diseases. The most common bodily symptom of chronic emotional blockage is joint pain, the energetic stagnation can easily find residence in the space in between bones. Another indication is hormonal disorder, if your hormone is imbalanced, it's likely because of your diet, lifestyle or just prolonged energy kink. That being said, we can regain hormonal balance by improving diet and smoothing out internal energy. Digestion is an immediate reflex on your nervousness. Many people have digestive problems right before an interview or exam, showing up as either can't eat or diarrhea.

Brain is the interface between emotion and body. But it is not the only place emotional energy shows up. As an emotion occurs, it happens in all soft tissues of the body, triggering a series of bodily reaction. However, bones are relatively unaffected by emotions, even the chronic ones. If we divide our body into two worlds, bones are on the side of consciousness, soft tissues and bio-electrons are on the side of manifestation. The most central bone in our body is the spine. It is the major residence of consciousness in a human form. Emotions can happen like crazy, body weight can be gained or lost, muscle density can be altered in months, nervous system can be reformed over a life time, but spine is never bothered by any of the biological movements.

Now let's take a look at the nervous system in the brain and spine. It's worth pointing out that there is another one in the intestines, which is very important on its own. But we will only include spine and brain in the discussion for now.

The nervous system in the brain can fluctuate in minutes. You can be in a good mood for one second, yet only turn into crying for the next few. For a masculine person, it is ridiculously amusing to look at a feminine person doing this. It's bizarre.

Of course, a more permanent neurological path in the brain can be formed over time. That's why we have developed our own thinking patterns and emotional patterns. We all have a few buttons that can trigger anger, fear, depression, and most likely, laughter. Every once in a while, we see something that reminds us of something in the past that is really funny. We laugh out loud completely out of context in other's eyes. That is a neurological mechanism being triggered.

Comparing to the brain, spine's neurology changes very little and over longer period. It's worth pointing out that the nervous system in the spine is not spine itself. The nerves attach onto spine, and function as an interface between the spine and the soft tissues as well as bioelectronics. When we talk about spine in the above, it's referred to the bones specifically. The complex integration between the bones of spine and the nerves on the bones is how consciousness interacts with the world.

Spine itself is human consciousness that can't be affected by thoughts and emotions, while nerves attached to it can. But these nerves in the spine are still less prone to re-programming, it is more primal and stable than the brain. We may feel headache over daily complexity. But only in very few significant moments, can we feel a tingling in the spine, if you are sensitive to energy.

A masculine person is more stable and less subjected to change, while a feminine person is changing mind and mood constantly. This is because the masculine person feels his spine more than the changing flesh, while the feminine person is more identified with energetic flow in the mind and body. They are both important to the whole, which consists of the clarity of awareness and the feeling of bodily existence. They have to both be there for a balance. The problem that an imbalanced Masculine results is boredom and death, while the problem that an imbalanced Feminine brings is chaos and psychotics. Neurology in the mind can be fucked up or pumped up both momentarily and chronically quite easy-and-fast. Yet the spinal nervous system is more intact with the unchanging embodiment of consciousness – the bones of spine, and therefore it's less reprogrammable. The mind of yours and that of a primitive tribal human's can be vastly different, but the nervous systems on both of your spines are evolved almost identically. Your mind pattern and that of the person sitting next to you on a train may have very little in common, as you were programmed differently by your past experiences. But you both would retract hands from a hot stove instantly with the same muscle movements. In fact, your spinal nervous system is very similar to that of a chimpanzee.

That being said, we now expand this realization to how we can offer love.

To love another person is to love her through the changing external conditions first, and then through the temporary mind patterns, and next to the nervous system on her spine which stays more or less the same ever since fully developed. Finally, we can love through the nerve domain to the bones. Just like the expression "I love you in my bones." Yes, it is literally to love her bones with yours, especially the spine in the center. It is a different feeling to love someone with a penis, a mind, a heart, a gut, and a spine, as it's best to do with all of them.

At the last stage, there's very minimum manifested form involved. Bones are the least part in the body that is subjected to change. Love is one consciousness recognizes itself in the other. It is to look through that person's appearing life situation, body features, mind patterns, emotional bundle, to who she really is as fundamental as this realm of human experience allows. It is a really beautiful thing to see someone you love as who she really is underneath all. It's a cosmetically erotic thing to commit to. The eternal porn.

Chapter 7:
The Matrix Has You

22.

Time Is the Source of Human Suffering

I dentification with time is the source of human suffering. We make a self image based on the past and project a future that our mind wants to control. Tension tightens with anticipation. Fear rushes in uncertainty.

Whatever rises will fall, and rise again as new. Humans can become either gross thinking mind or subtle inner being. We certainly are not our thoughts, nor an entity of past residue. We only appear to be here as an entity of being, part of which is condensed into physical bodies. Yet who we are at depth is stretched even before this birth and after our death, ever more permanent than either physical forms or inner beings. Whenever you become the witness of all movements, not letting desire or trauma take over or act through, you fall into total freedom.

Thoughts are monsters. And space is the only freedom that can contain it. By floating thoughts mid-air, mind can do no more damage. Being rooted in this moment as the formless self is the gateway to un-manifested space.

If earth is devoid of human life, there would be no concept of time. Civilization is built upon rationality and thinking, which necessitates time. Meanwhile, a jungle is growing by being there as what it is, which can only happen in the moment. We usually let strategies take control of us. Yet as you forget the concept of time, there is no longer an uncontrollable future bundled with the past. Without time, suffering can no longer fit in.

23.

Hamster's Adventure

A well-lived life isn't about happiness. Think about enlightened human beings throughout history. Few had a "happy" life. Jesus was crucified, Gandhi was abstinent. As men, we're here to find our cross and be willingly crucified by a force beyond human effort. It may require you to be happy, may require you to never talk, may require you to have lots of sex, or to never have sex. What you need to do is to feel the current of entirety underneath all seemingly separate events as much as you can. And trust it until you're no longer in fear.

You might not be ready for this step. It's totally fine. There isn't one choice better than others but only honest ones. Even our need to secure a good life is a tip of the surface wave from the deep current. When we are young, we try to get something for ourselves, money, power, women. Some of us do get what we want but only realize that no amount of money, power or women can bring lasting security. It's just the same internal conflicts reoccurring in another context. There seems always something urgent to our attention. So we start to look around for people doing worse than us, maybe starting with our unsuccessful relatives. We try to help them grow a business or even give them a business, hoping them to succeed. We get into a reality of helping others. It is a much more noble attitude, but is still driven by mind's need to occupy on *something*. Without being aware of it, we secretly want to feel whole and fulfilled by shifting effort to others' problems from our own. Through such noble act, our hearts open a little. We no longer act as a separate thing slashing through a jungle made of individuals who are just about to do the same to us. Your heart grows bigger as personal tension loosens.

Eventually, you realize that just like your own life wasn't made perfect by pursuing, neither were those of the people you tried to help. Maybe they wasted opportunities for the lack of discipline. Maybe they weren't as motivated as you were. Or, maybe the business you gave them did take off well, and a few years later this relative indulges in a destructive lifestyle and becomes addicted to drugs. Then you wonder whether he would be happier if I didn't try to help at all. Or, is changing other's life situation even wise or dis-balancing?

You might be donating wealth and time to support a town in less-developed country, only to find out that crime rate rockets as population grows bigger. People that you set out to help have tasted greed, meanwhile the amount of people killed by murder has just exceeded that by starvation before you came along. Now what?

You wanted a nice car and a big house when you were a teenager. Then you sat in a big house alone wishing you have a wife to take care of. The perfect relationship settled into routine after the honeymoon. Now looking at those lives that you set out to help, yours and others', it all changed but nothing has fundamentally improved, yours or theirs. You throw away the business suit. "This is it." Nothing I gain or lose will have a substantial effect on me or the world. The only substantiality was there in the beginning and is here now. All I can choose is to realize it now or to finish *Dadada* first. And I have to make the choice every time I start to hope and fear again. I will let the whole thing transform itself, and watch it without interference. Nothing needs to be done. Just one thing needs to be realized. And it took us decades of running around to see it.

To stabilize the feeling of truth takes endless discipline. But in fact, you should consider yourself extremely blessed just to have the karma or constellation to be aware that there might be something beyond the hamster wheel. The majority of population have yet to experience that there are something more permanently cool than cashing a pay check and shopping.

If people can see how their life end up with, they might want to kill themselves. Beyond the promise from Target commercials featuring a stoned family going shoplifting, there isn't much that we have learned to live for. Perhaps nobody has ever showed us how to be a human, let alone how to be a male human.

Here we have the three stages: the first stage wants a muscle car for himself so that he's cooler than everyone else. The second stage wants everyone to have a muscle car, so that we are all cool. The third stage realizes that I might never be able to fill the world with muscle cars, and people might not even want a muscle car, and if I give everyone a muscle car then it won't be cool anymore. So why bother from the start. It seems all a mirage to get you running. And hamsters are very delighted to run this cage. It seems a promising journey worth attending to, doesn't it?

In the third stage, you realize that the need for control is trivial and rigid, in the end certainly insignificant. You let go of all boundaries that promise you security. You are absolutely transparent to the entirety that swirls as everything appearing. You act in whatever way that transmits truth in the world, not through analyzing, but with intuitive response to a situation. It may look like that you have successfully created a comfortable life, or you have become a homeless guy playing guitar under a bridge. It may require you to live happily with many women and children, or staying celibate and alone in a cave.

The right action is never up to your preference. But when you are doing it, it feels right. There are people that feel wrong for having a few million dollars. For some people, an out-of-blue sense of guilt, a psychological resistance of materials, an un-fill-able need to accumulate and a distant relationship with personal belongings might come from wealth. But for some, a wealthy life is their way to express freedom. You are allowing a right-ness to live through you. All your life's arrangements are for the sake of enlarging the expression of truth, like a balloon being inflated with puffy authenticity. To the hamsters, it might seem that you have ruined your cage or have mastered it. But only you can feel when and what is right.

We have to stop bullshitting ourselves. If a relational arrangement or a business situation doesn't feel right, if your intuition is feeling *Urhhhhh*, don't pretend and cope. Don't self talk and rationalize. It is wrong and you know it instantly. So stop the bullshit and get the fuck out.

When you are no longer adding the layer of fear resulting as personal preference and avoidance, it's up to you to interact with a situation and to be led to what expresses your unique shape of truth.

There are a thousand and one ways to live truth. It appears very different in each human being. Look at the figures that we love – Jesus, Gandhi, Batman, Rock Star, Rocky Balboa, Your Grandmother. Each transmits the same truth in his or her own ways. Rich or poor, celebrated or crucified, fictional or lived, they express the truth that we deep down know, but are too fearful to feel, too lazy to live out. Through their expression, we feel the one brave heart that has been covered up by our conditioned mind. If you love them or any other characters, living or dead, invented or real, he or she is in you already. That's why you are attracted to their way of living truth. That quality in your hero is what you already have but are too afraid to live. Once in a while someone comes along. They inspire us to tears. They trigger the chord of our soul to resonate. Your mission of this life is to find that chord and don't let it die before you do.

24.

The Amusement of Nightmares

For most men, to be absolutely transparent to their life's purpose requires formal periods of solitude. Meditate 30 minutes a day, a week in the wilderness, or even sailing across the ocean alone. Approaches may vary, but it often happens when you are comfortably free-falling in nothingness. Facing a white wall for a day, motivation will rise from your gut.

This is a daunting look at your life if you are not ready for it. The sense of identity that you spent years to build has to be let go of. You have been convincing yourself that you are special and your life story is leading to somewhere significant. To allow truth to live through you is to realize that you are not special or even separate. Any confidence built upon identity has a limit, but only confidence that is rooted in death has no fear. Death is the empty spacious capacity that contains all life. Getting lost in life's changing pictures, we forget death. Looking away from death, we become afraid, as if external events threatens our existence.

You have nothing to lose, because you have nothing to begin with. Nothing belongs to you but the capacity to witness. Everything happening is the dance of universe. You are watching it now, even though you often forget that you are watching it. You are not happening, only your flesh and thoughts and emotions are rising, under the watch of someone, who is the only thing you can possibly be. Your body lives without your control. Blood circulates without your thinking. Metabolism, inhalation, heartbeat, emotions, you are not doing it. Nature is taking care of it. Your body is just a piece of rotting meat. Your mind streams like crazy even after years of meditation. The good thing is that you are not your body or mind at all. You are the knowing of everything that is happening. And that knowing, has no limits.

We can relate this reality we are in to a dream. When you are dreaming, events in the dream have significant importance, until you wake up, or until you think you wake up. Then you are here, believing the urgency and necessities in the real world, where you chase one thing after another just like how you did in dreams. Most people believe that our reality is solid – tables, careers, relationships. The truth is, any reality is just a fluid jelly. There is no solidity ever. Everything is moving and changing. A dream reality is often more unstable than that we are used to – a table can transform into a room all of a sudden. In the current reality, table's transformation is too slow to be noticed. But careers do end and marriages do become lawsuits. That you noticed. Your resistance to this fluid nature in this or any dream, is your suffering. A table becomes a room. It can be a fun phenomenon to watch or a scary nightmare to escape from. Depends on how much you can let go of the false assumption of solidity. Depends on how long you can still remember that you are in a dream.

25.

The Paradox of Hope

ope is something illusory if we are really honest. But hope can give us intense presence in this moment, as we believe in achieving something in the future. When hope brings us presence, it becomes an useful tool. In effect, hope has power. That power exists right here, instead of in an imaginary future.

Here is the scene. Hope doesn't have real value in itself. But once it creates the communication between us and the is-ness, it is valuable. It is paradoxical as most discussions of truth are. When you are obsessed about being present, you are awkwardly forcing yourself into a fixed state according to a remembered experience. This forcefulness is often futile, as presence often happens spontaneously.

How do you have it happen rather than to conform yourself to the concept of meditation?

Here, many seeming useless illusions become the target for you to shoot. By aiming at a target out there, you are panoramically aware right here. Without them, we are just pretending to be aiming but not doing it for real. That target, is hope.

The beginning of meditation is to see through the futile gesture of hope and passion. But as you have experienced meditation, we have a choice to stay still or to move. In fact, we don't really have the options. We are in motion as long as we remain human. You have to eat, drink, breathe, pee and shit, allow blood to circulate, and probably deal with the environment, culture and people.

We can't be absolutely away from illusions. This is a realm of illusion and you are a part of it. And this realization makes the illusory world as solid and real as it can get. You are truth coming through an illusory form in a grand illusion. For your human experience, whatever right here is the most real thing this realm can offer.

Now knowing that movements are inevitable, the question is how you should move to express truth. People either go to one extreme of ignorance or the other. Most never realize who they are as indestructible truth. For the few that realized it, they attempt to negate their bodily existence.

Hope and passion are worthless in realizing who you are. But hope can also be the bright target for you to aim at. What's the point of aiming? In order shoot. And what's more important, the action of aiming or the result of shooting? You should know that a perfect shot never exist in life. Life is an ongoing imperfection. But even though we don't take result as an objective, the process towards result can bring us to a state of focus in front of that target called perfection. The state of focus is the knowing of who you are. Now dare you say again that targets are just useless illusions?

The key here is to believe your hope. In fact, it's better to not know anything that I just described up there. Once you know that hope is illusory, you are likely no longer convinced to aim at the target. It's better to just aim at the damn thing and determine to shoot without knowing the ultimate truth. The direct relationship with the target will bring you to focus either you know it or not. In fact, if your goal is to match a certain state of focus instead of to purely hit target, you probably can't be a good shooter or aimer.

So what do we do now?

First, we realize that hope is unnecessary, because the only truth is right now. Then we see the utilitarian value of it. Next, very importantly, we come to forget its unnecessity and practical use altogether. Now you can have your hope impeccably, while maintaining a direct communication with the present situation in sensitivity.

Therefore, forget all that you know. Even the ultimate truth which is the reality of existence. Forget about it like everything else. Just look at that target and get yourself to shoot like a soldier following orders. Truth is something to be, not to think about and then match yourself to. Shoot the damn thing and then you become truth, right here.

Everything has its place. Realization, hope, passion, and even analysis. Analysis is trivial. But without certain amount of it, we can hardly bring any spontaneous impulse into real-world existence. Hope and passion are futile play. But they can be used to truth's advantage of expressing love. Sometimes the opposite of being present in right now is what brings us to right now. There we have it. Forget everything I just told you, and shoot the fucking thing now.

Chapter 8:
Hard Lessons for Men

26.

Integrity
and Spiritual ED

*A man must be able to differentiate either it is to lie
out of compassion or out of ego.*

Integrity is not something you can afford to sacrifices even just a little. Once you lose some of it, you lose all of it. As a man, your career, your creation, your body and mind should be all sourced in this integrity. Personal power is authentic and forceful without hesitation or hiding, only when all your actions, thoughts and words are sourced from your integrity.

It's tempting to give in on integrity in minor ways because it looks like a good business opportunity. Yet if you sacrifices integrity for any personal benefits, the whole structure starts to collapse. Consequently, you feel uncertain with your career, uninspired in your art, lack of confidence in the world. Every masculine identified man should have his one craft that he pours his heart into. He will give up everything including his personal well-being, his life, or even the woman of his love to this one thing. This is his art. And nothing else matter outside of it. Without integrity, he can't create art. To devote into art is to offer your whole-hearted integrity to your craft. If your integrity has collapsed, you have no real power. You can fake it, but it can't create art.

There are men who are satisfied with less. Earning a living with lies, they live their entire life with fabricated mental reality. Their confidence has to depend on something outside, a trophy wife, a nice car, a big house, a glamorous position. Hiding under those possessions they gained by manipulating, they are afraid. They are afraid of losing the trophy wife or nice car. They know that they are worthless without possessions. Losing integrity won't affect them much, because they don't have much to begin with. Their structure is built externally while an honest man grows he's spine internally.

A man can lose everything, but never his integrity. It is the foundation of all our artistic creations and relationships. Without it, nothing powerful will come from you, either an intention or an ejaculation.

Integrity is your dick. It is infinitely big, and has the power to create, penetrate and crush the world. A man who sells his integrity is like a woman who sells her pussy. Only different being a woman will still have a pussy after selling it, but you won't have any once you lose your dick.

If a woman catches her boyfriend ever strategize to lie either in business or friendship, she should immediately dump him. You are virtually dating a man with no dick. If you ever find your friend or business partner lying to anyone, watch out because sooner or later you will be involved too.

Integrity is a structure. One column's gone and the entire building collapse. You can always choose to not say, but any lie you tell will diminish your personal power.

Without that integrity to support all you actions, you struggle in clarity, precision and certainty. If you are an honest man that sources your career, creation and relationships from your integrity, telling a small lie in business can even affect your concentration in the gym or determination on a rock climbing trip. And that, is threatening.

27.

Hard Dick, Soft Heart

Consciousness can come through a good heart. But a good heart alone is not necessarily conscious. The cultivation for men is on the one hand of awareness, and on the other hand of heart. A heart can be the most powerful vehicle for consciousness to manifest through.

Often times, a woman follows you because you are cool, not because you have a good heart. As humans, it's worth cultivating a good heart rather than a bad one. As masculine beings, it becomes a responsibility to be cool. Women and the world will like or love your heart, but until you are cool, she won't trust you. To bring love to the world, you have no choice but to erect rock-hard in one way or another.

Cool is a representation of masculinity. Masculinity is the ability to remain conscious amidst of all change. To illustrate, let's take a look at things considered cool by a wide range of beliefs. Those things are: muscle, money, social connection, success, charisma, presence.

All of the above are representations of consciousness. If you are a man living in a jungle, having muscle means that you can force your consciousness into the tribe with muscular strength.

After money was invented, you can now hire people for their physical force. You can pay for a big guy to force your consciousness into the group. When you hire enough big guys, you get yourself an army.

Meanwhile, social connection means your ability to have others do labor for you. The more connections you have, the easier it is for you to put your will to reality. They represent you ability to press consciousness through external forms.

Next is success. Besides the ability to utilize others' labor force. Success reflects one's capacity to stay on course. We are in a world of change. To have any enterprise or any valuable work done, you have to stay on a path through the changing mind and external conditions. This ability to be on track is the ability to stay conscious among distractions. Women love money just like men love women's breasts. No matter how evolved a meditator you are, when a pair of upright juicy boobs are at your face, there will be a reflective response to that youthful bouncy jello. Here goes the other way, no matter how evolved a woman is, the immediate responses to a billionaire and his broke twin brother are different. She can of course train herself not to judge men by wealth, just like we can educate ourselves to not judge a woman by appearance. But the primal reaction is still deep in our nervous system inherited way back from hairy ancestors.

When a woman sees a jacked wolverine in the mall, there will be a primal jolt. A wolverine was everything a woman needs to survive and raise children before civilization. And in evolution, we haven't gone very far from it.

Now you might have see the sequence on the scale. Muscle, money, success, charisma, presence. It goes higher on the scale from muscle to presence. Of course there's more inter-connection among those characteristics, such as that a fit man will be able to express presence through his body, evoking others' trust emotionally. But for now, let's just look at the direct representative value of them.

Presence is the root quality of a man who can stay calm, make a plan and get shit done. If there's a fire in the building, a more conscious person will have a clear thinking to figure out an escape plan. This is the value of presence in a practical sense.

All types of masculine sexiness have something to do with consciousness, either the capacity to press it into the world, the implication of this capacity, or a direct transmission of it. A less evolved cave women will be attracted to a man with physical strength. All women love wolverine for certain amount, but a more evolved women might likely to choose a less jacked James Bond. If a woman is self-sufficient and successful, though she might still have a primal jolt towards a bodybuilder or a billionaire, she will be more attracted to a man's depth.

Everyone should have a good heart, some people are karmically more in touch with it, others need cultivation to let it out. In fact, our good heart only starts to recoil after being betrayed by the world. It is an extremely important task to remain our heart open and tender. This is our responsibility as humans.

Yet again, no matter how good of a heart you have. No woman or world will follow your guidance simply because of it. It's a good add-on to have in terms of sexual attraction, but sadly, an unnecessary one. Women are sexual beings. For men, our sexual experience is localized at the genital region and the fantasizing head. For a woman, her entire body and subtle being is a sexual organ. She experiences sex with the whole body and subtle emotional entity, while we pump our way to a funny burst of sperm. Men's sex is quite pathetic if remain localized.

A woman trusting a man with her emotions, it is sex in action on the subtle level. She is light, and is attracted to consciousness. There is a scale of light just like a scale of consciousness. A bimbo fake-boob babe goes with inflated wealth. A woman devoted to love will attract a man present as space. Space wants to contain light, and light needs a space to shine. A woman can shine with her boobs, her mind, her emotions and her heart. That attracts her counterpart.

Having a good heart is totally enough. But if you want a feminine partner to experience truth with, you will need to demonstrate consciousness. When you are consciousness, your presence will come out to the world through your good heart. That is your practice as a human and as a man.

Chapter 9:
Love
is the Substance

28.

Enlightenment and Love

Love is the union between consciousness and light.
The intertwinement between consciousness and
luminance is happening in all experiences. In other
words, anytime you are experiencing anything at
all – a view, a sound, a thought, consciousness is
doing light. The doing is so intense that they unite
as one melting happening, with no sense of sep-
arateness. Love is happening, and to meditate is to
formally practice feeling this ultimate truth of con-
sciousness and luminance.

Enlightenment is to love. When you tried all practices to meditate but still can't feel the truth you know, switch them around. Feel love first, and then you can't help but be meditating.

Meditation is impossible without feeling love's absolute. It results in love, and also *is* the experience of love.

Only when you can love one person, with no demand or necessity or need, are you capable of loving anything. The feeling of loving one person in the midst of all things dying is the same feeling of loving everything and everyone. If you want to learn to meditate or to feel your heart more, then love your most-loved person without expecting anything in return. Everything will be taken away, everyone will leave you. Love prevails.

To love is to give all of you without the slightest need for anything to be in certain way.

It's all going to be ok. Even not ok is ok.

Don't withdraw when the situation is unpleasant. Love is the nature of everything and every experience. Only when we confuse love with needs, can we be hurt. Then we are afraid of feeling the hurt. Instead of recoiling, we shall stay with the pain, love and breathe the pain, give all of you to it as if the hurt itself is your lover. As emotion dissolves inevitably just like everything else, you know love for absolute. Nothing to need, nothing to fear. You are loving everything appearing, with the same intensity of offer to your most loved person. It's a constant adventure as love continues.

Your darkest shame and guilt, sense of inadequacy, all the imperfection that you wish to fix. Love all imperfections. Love your guilt and regrets, with the same intense love you can ever give to your lover as if it's the last instant you will ever see her. We will all die. Giving in every instant, with whatever condition you end up with, is the only way to live and die. A perfect life is one that you have given every thing you can to offer to one person and to everyone, without fear for future, because you might die right now. To offer your love even across great distance, either she knows you or forgets you as forms dissolve. Whatever you end up with, there you are. The only choice we have for now and ever, is to hide or to offer.

The world is beautiful. Yet it is your lover in hurt. You either stand up showing her that everything will be ok because you are here with her, or keep being an asshole postponing your love under all kinds of excuses that will be forever present. You will never be a perfect saint as long as you remain human. We are fucked up and will continue being so if not further. Love can't wait. Your offering can't wait. Feel you urge to offer. Feel your love to the person you love the most. Stay with the same intensity and offer it now. Things will come and go.

Fear is at odds with love. When you love intensely, fear goes out of focus. When you are no longer wrapped in mental calculation, fear has nowhere to be. When you give immensely like a river, there is nothing that you can't afford to lose. Don't wait. You will die one day, possibly in any second.

29.

The Only Commitment

People grow, relationships change. Therefore we don't commit to a person or a relationship. We only commit to what's absolute, what's always there. We only commit to the fundamental truth of love. We do whatever will magnify love for all. When your commitment is to love one person, both personal preference and relational arrangements are put aside. If a time comes when your absence brings her more openness than your attentiveness can, you will have to let her go, but you will be faithful to your commitment. When someone else can join her to create more inspiration, you might have to sacrifices your hope of personal good life for the greater love.

In fact, you have to let go constantly. You do not stop loving. Love continues deepen even when bodies drift apart. You give your deepest love in the midst of togetherness or separation, happiness and hurts. At the same time, let go moment by moment. Let it all dissolve as it happens. Let love have its way, even if it means to ruin your personal good life.

If the day comes when your lover falls into someone else. Let her go and give her your blessing. This is your chance to prove how much you love her.[1]

Nothing will change if you don't know how to love. Nothing will change if you know how to love, except that you know how to love.[2]

Only very few people are willing to stand in love's hurt without closure or withdrawal. To give love when loved is easy. True practice is to love without fear when rejected. It takes practice to remain open without recoil. However, even though you commit to love regardless of your self interest, how would you know what to do is the right course to magnify love for all? This is when art comes in, like a good sailor can sense an upcoming weather change, and feel what the right action is.

To absolutely trust love is to let go of all holdings for self protection and security. You are free falling.

This place is not about happiness. 100 years from now, we are all going to die. Nothing ever mattered and nothing will ever matter. The only difference is either you die fully given or die still holding back in fear.

---

1   Osho, *Love, Freedom, Aloneness*, 2001

2   David Deida, *Instant Enlightenment*, 2007

Happiness is not something to go to, but to go *through*.

Ultimately, there is no relationship. But you can set up commitments as the context for discipline, for the sake of both you and others. You have to know exactly why you choose her, beyond the need for home, and make that active choice every single day. You are not worthy of anyone if you just happen to stay with her for the momentum of comfort.

Let go and then give all. What worse can happen?

30.

To Love Everything
Is to Love Your Woman

Women are all around you. There is a force of nature that is attractive to perception, the force that grows trees, blossoms flowers, moves the ocean and lights up a woman. That is the force of life, of all light and appearance.

She can never be apart from you, but only appear and come through as the changing forms. The same love that unguards your heart when your woman smiles is the force that moves the leaves on trees. You don't have to be with her to love her. To love a woman is to love everything around you, everyone and every situation. Appearing pictures may be good or bad, but underneath it is your woman's fluid nature that moves all and lives as all.

Bodies drift apart. Love stays right here. Experiences will not be if consciousness and light part ways. As long as perception lasts, you are always with her.

The world could be a dream or a hallucination. What's outside of this room may or may not be there. All you ever have is this room and every room that you happen to be in. All she can be is as the rooms. When she is here, you can love her. When she is not here, you love her as everything and everyone that is here. Because they are her, you are her. Every sensation is her move as difference appearances. It might be momentarily comforting or destructing. But it is the one love that lives all.

If you can love a person, you can love the world as it is. Because the world as it is is that person, that can never die or leave, even long after our bodies dissolve.

Chapter 10:
Awaken from Dysfunction

31.

Emotions are Energy

Every emotion is a flavor of energy. There's no good or bad. Emotional energies are like colors, some are green, some are red. Some are more pleasant than others. But we don't assume green is good and red is bad. Great art can come through either one.

Transmutation of emotion can bring you calmness. But you don't have to transmute it to access peace. Peace is the space that contains you and me as well as your emotion my emotion. When you are excited, the space is there; when you are agonized, the space doesn't change. To have peace is to access peace amidst of pleasure and pain. In fact, you are always at peace. We are just so used to ignore this fact, *where* we really are.

Next time when you have an overwhelming emotion, to an extend that you can vividly feel it in your physical body, you can choose to witness it happening without grasping or covering up the feeling of sorrow with entertainment or conversation. In the movie *Fight Club*, Tyler burns the narrator's hand – *"stay with the pain, this is the most glorious moment of your life"* .

Eventually everything goes away, including your most excruciating hurt. By that time you can't have it back even if you want to. So use the energy of pain or pleasure while you have it. Don't hide, don't run, don't grab. Stay with it, because *it is a glorious moment of your life*. Whenever you can stay with an emotion without screaming in resistance, you have found peace. Peace is always present, even when you are being burnt. It's just hard to remember when pleasure or pain becomes unbearable.

Energy can be leaked through conversation, entertainment, ejaculation or even thinking. Enjoyment of life has its value. But we tend to use it as a diversion of attention so that we can avoid feeling pain and loneliness. This diversion tactic is not evil by all means, just mediocre. Once you are addicted to entertainment, talking, and ejaculation, you won't have any idea how much energy you have wasted. Yet if you stop ejaculating for a while, the amount of focus and clarity you can have will shock you. Only with abundant energy can you realize that even talking and eating junk food are jeopardizing your spiritual depth as well as mental acuity.

When the hurt or pleasure burns intensely, try to channel that energy down through the front to the base of your body with your breath, instead of letting it tighten your neck, chest or stomach. Then intentionally direct it upwards through your back along the spine. Circulate that energy, and then you harvest it. Internal energy is stored in your lower belly when not in use. Whenever it gets stuck in the frontal body, you can circulate it with intention and then channel it back to the battery at lower belly. Energy flows naturally down through the front and up through the spine. Breathing deep can release the felt-pressure of heavy chest or tightened face. Intentionally sealing the pelvic floor and pulling it upwards while exhale can pressure energy up to and over the top of head. Then circulate downward again with another inhalation. Kegel exercise done after giving birth is the medical term of this energy yoga.

Remember, despair is not less than happiness. They are both usable energies, which can be circulated at use, or stagnate to harm.

Anger, despair and feeling of futility can very well be used in physical training and competitive sports such as boxing, as effectively as motivation can do.

You have a choice to live as an artist. Every type of energy you can feel is just a flavor of color, some more intense than others, but all are usable to paint your unique masterpiece. In the hand of Vincent Van Gogh, even the flavor of suicide can be painted into beauty that inspires life.

32.

How to Rebuild Happiness After Breakup

_Energy, Health, and Meditation

There are three aspects in regard to happiness: emotional health, flow of energy, and enlightenment. They solve specific problems and work together as a whole. Emotional health and flow of energy coexist and affect each other. Enlightenment leads to the realization that nothing is ever necessary. Enlightenment helps you loosen the obsession, let go of fear, and have better sex, all of which contribute to the other two aspects.

Rebuild Happiness and Personal Power:

When we use the word happiness, we are referring to the unobstructed flow of energy. There are two approaches to make energy flow:

- One is to stimulate the generating process, so that energy moves through your body with greater force.
- The other is to clear the blockage in your body, so that energy flows smoothly.

The addition to both is to circulate energy so that it doesn't leak out. It's rare for a man to learn to circulate high energy inside of his body, not leaking through ejaculation, fidgeting, excessive talking or unnecessary thinking. When a man hasn't been ejaculating for a while, internal energy builds up. Your urge to ejaculate intensifies. You tap your legs unconsciously; you can't sit still; your mindstream doesn't stop. When you are a teenager, your energy renews fast. Excessive ejaculation or tapping your heels at dinner table doesn't appear to have negative effects on your well-being. But you might have had a deep sense of depletion right after masturbation. You then become irritable, lacking of humor, seeing the world against you. Your eyes look like those on a dead fish. The project that turns you on suddenly becomes uninteresting.

To be happy is to have high energy flow in your body. Although circulation is not necessary in terms of just being happy, channeling energy without leakage will give you massive personal power. Power is ultimately the capacity to bring love to every situation through every gesture. To cultivate personal power, you will need abundant energy and the capacity to channel this energy with your intention. Intention leads internal energy to flow throughout your body. Energy is built up as the fuel to perform the speech, movement and venture.

Circulate Sexual Energy:
In case you haven't realize, internal energy is sexual energy. As you grow older, the regeneration of energy slows down. To maintain erection when you are an old man, you need to circulate without leaking. This doesn't mean to not have sex, but to convert your localized pudendal-nerve orgasm into a whole-body orgasm, by channeling your built-up sexual energy from the genital up through spine.

Our bodies are not used to sustain high internal energy. When your sexual energy builds up, it often gets stuck in your head causing sexual fantasies, or in your genitals urging you to ejaculate. Mostly both. You will be very uncomfortable and horny if this energy is not circulated throughout your whole body. When you finally ejaculate, you have a sense of release. We all know how pleasurable it is. Sometimes it's rejuvenating if energy is fluidly exchanged through sex. But besides the exchange of sexual energy, the pleasurable sense of release comes with depletion. High energy is what makes you passionate about your woman and your work. The moment it's drained, you suddenly lose interest in woman's naked body or the project that is true to your heart. You lose erection after ejaculation, for your woman and the world. The passion in foreplay is gone. All you want to do is to roll to the other side, sleep. Excessive ejaculation makes you mediocre. It's your loss.

Energy Blockage Caused by Emotional Wound:
As mentioned in the beginning, happiness is the unobstructed flow of high energy. Most people only discover that stimulation can boost up their energy, and therefore make them happy. So you hang out with friends, go to a movie, karaoke, eat a oversized ice-cream. All those have their place in happiness, but if you abuse these stimuli, or if you don't know how to circulate the over-dozed energy, it's like poring concrete into an abysmal expecting filling it up, or even worse, energy can become blocked. That's when all your movies, friends, karaokes and ice-creams stop working.

No matter how much energy you stimulate, if it doesn't flow, you stay depressed. A blockage is formed anytime you act in reaction of fear, fear of not getting or fear of losing. As your life continues, you get wounded one way or another. You know it, regardless of how happy you appear on facebook. These abuse issues develop into kinks in our body. A sexual abuse is not just referring to being beaten by boyfriend. When you wrote that letter to the girl in fourth grade, and she cut it in front of the class, good luck spending ten years to remove that kink. Next decade every time you see a pair of scissors, the frontal part of your body contracts. All flow stops.

Every time your open heart hits closure, you develop a wound. That wound hardens into a blockage in your body. Over time, you become increasingly fearful, developing shells to protect yourself from being hurt. One way to measure the strength of your practice is of your capacity to remain relaxedly vulnerable in pain or pleasure, without contraction.

All emotional problems are bodily problems. All emotional reactions are bodily reactions to your thoughts. When you're emotionally hurt, the frontal part of your body collapses. When you feel stress, energy is locked in the head around your eyes. Then your mind and face tense up in fear. The kinks in your body are being triggered by thoughts. Once activated, they block the flow of internal energy. Together with the leakage through excessive thinking, your energy depletes. This depletion is reflected in your every move. Everyone around you can feel it.

Live as a Gift through Your Emotional Wound:
No one is immune from these kinks and wounds. Throughout your life, your purpose is to give yourself completely as a gift to the world and the women. Essentially they are the same. The world is a less condensed form of woman. This giving is art. You will always feel inadequate. Therefore, it's important to remember the nature of existence moment by moment, so that in every instant either we give our presence fully or not, either our art is right on or far off, we know that ultimately nothing matters. From time to time, you will get hurt because your heart is vulnerably open. That's when you have to put

aside art, to heal. Once healed, you carry on giving yourself, until you get wounded again.

The opposite of this is to develop a shell once being hurt. You close down your heart and act through a shell. This closure causes a much more fundamental suffering. Holding back eventually becomes most people's life story. A good rock climber makes every leap with every cell of their being. That is their art of climbing. And that's how you should treat your art of giving. Nothing will make you happier than to offer your gift that you are born to give.

Meditation Leads to Enlightenment, NOT Happiness:
Meditation doesn't make you happy. It makes you realize that happiness is not a necessity. This feeling realization is threatening. We are all too afraid of sitting still and alone.

Meditation is not therapeutic at all. No amount of meditation can remove your kinks. Its function – if there is one at all – is to help you recognize that nothing matters, or even exists. In the process, you don't care about your kinks. You are complete and perfect even with all the wounds. You become like the Steven Hawking, as external limits no longer bind you. You eventually reach another level of happiness: nothing needs to be done; what ever is, is as is. Meditative practice is to recognize the empty nature of the universe: everything is just a spontaneous appearing picture. You watch your thoughts come and go like a fire bursts and dies, until there's absolutely nothing. Everything dissolves, quite orgasmatically.

Once you access the depth of ocean through meditation, the surface storm becomes a ripple.

So is it true that all your problems can be solved through meditation?

No. Nothing is solved by sitting still. But you certainly realize that nothing needs to be solved. If you don't eat, you will die. But if you die, so what? Meditation is to recognize the reality of existence. It doesn't solve your problems, but makes you realize that your problems don't need to be solved. Solve your shit or not, we are all gonna die. A hundred years later you will end up in the dirt. In fact, you might be dead already but just don't know it yet.

Some practitioners moved to a cave, meditating for lifetime to sustain the pristine awareness of death. However a true master can always access this death-like emptiness even when his dick is being sucked. A master practitioner is not distracted by pleasure, and therefore he is not afraid of pleasure. He is not grasping life's appearing stories, and therefore he is not afraid of life. In an orgy or in pain, do not narrow your attention.

Spiritual recognition is instantaneous. In this moment, you either feel the empty nature of everything or not yet. When you do, you realize that even happiness is just an appearance, dissolving as it happens. As a result, you're *happy* because nothing needs to be done or avoid.

The challenge is to sustain this recognition. For a moment you realize that nothing needs to be done. However, the very next moment you remember that your rent is due. Maintaining the feeling of freedom while you pay your rent is the practice. Sourced from the knowing of death, the practice is to remain free, non-grasping and present when a woman is sucking your dick, or leaving you.

Spiritual awakening is essentially letting go of all holdings and security, knowing death, yet not afraid of life. This brings you beyond happiness, even if your energy is not flowing.

Enlightenment seems to be the answer to all human problems. But it is not the end. You are born as human, so that you can give love even as a fucked-up. A rock can't do it. You can't do it after you die. You can be an enlightened monk or an enlightened stripper. The later brings a-thousand-fold more love to this world.

Clear Emotional Blockage:
When you have emotional wound, high energy will be blocked in certain region of your body. This discomfort urges you to ejaculate. Ejaculation depletes your energy, so that nothing is left to be stagnated afterwards. The problem is that the wound is still there, and now you are emptied out. You then will need to ejaculate on a frequency. Ejaculation can solve your discomfort caused by blockage, but leaves you mediocre and depressed.

This is when you tell your friends that your life is fucked by bitches.

There are two ways to remove the kinks and wounds. What do you do when your toilet blocks? You may choose to:

- flush it with more water;
- or remove the blockage.

Flushing is called yoga; removing is called therapy. Yoga is to facilitate circulation with bodily movement, in order to flush energy channels; therapy is to operate on the wound directly.

Therapy is very efficient in removing the emotional response to past experiences. It tunes down your tendency to collapse when past hurt is triggered. Therapy doesn't necessarily make your happy, but it creates the condition for energy to flow freely.

The other way to do therapy is through talking to friends. You talk, they listen. That's all. Don't construct stories based on memory, but just share feelings. The more you put experience into a story, the more you make yourself a victim. This is to have your friend as a therapist. I wouldn't recommend you to put shit onto other individuals often. But once in a few years should be tolerable, as you will do the same for them one day. Remember to have some humor for the other person. It's best to have a trustable female friend for such support. Men friends often bypass the blockage issue into a macho go-hunting-on-Saturday digression, which could be good for the spirit, but not for health. You are extremely lucky if you have friends that understand what you are going through and are willing to spend hours to hear you talking. Thank your friends.

Next we'll talk about yoga. Yoga has nothing to do with enlightenment. We don't become enlightened merely because we do very good yoga. On the other hand, many spiritually enlightened people are yogic-ly blocked. Again, enlightenment is to know that nothing matters, including yogic flow, even though you can be conscious and energetically flowing at the same time.

The word yoga represents everything that facilitates the flow of energy, from traditional yoga, Tai Chi, playing guitar, listening to R&B, painting, creating your art, exchange energy with people. Everything makes you flow more smoothly is yoga.

Yoga has two basic functions. First is to help clear out the blockage or wound. It's not as direct as therapy, but is a good addition. The second function is to make flow of your built-up energy. That is happiness.

Clear Emotional Blockage through Sex:
One way to clear out blockage is the exchange of sexual energy, from flirting to good sex. Good sex in this context means sexual energy flowing through multiple bodies. Intercourse or not, hearts have to connect for energy exchange. Two things to be careful of: first is that sex itself may trigger you response to past wound, if you just caught your wife with another dude; second is that you shouldn't ejaculate, otherwise your body is un-blocked but your energy is gone.

The way to not ejaculate is to feel into the other's body more than your own. Feel the placement of her legs and ankles, how does it feel like to have the weight of breasts bouncing, what's the rhythm and depth of breathing. Do it as a first-person-view perception, not a technique. A start to feel her is to synchronize your inhalation and exhalation with hers. You subtle being will synchronize once breath is in unison. Feel her very intensely to a point where she is your world, where you don't even notice how you feel as you disappear like everything else. You ride her pleasure instead of focusing on yours. Women's pleasure is always more over-flowing than yours. Letting go of yourself, feel her completely and feel the entirety of the room. Simultaneously, feel beyond the room as far as you can. Feel that there are people on earth that can't feed themselves, whose family has just been murdered, or who is suffering excruciating pain of dying, and you are having sex rather than taking time to help them. If you are choosing to fuck, then fuck to magnify love. You are pumping as love's pulse, transmitting love to your woman, into the world, to every body that is suffering.

Good sex helps you circulate energy and flushes out your emotional blockage. Do it or not, remember not to ejaculate. Depletion is another word for depression.

33.

From Cuddling to BDSM

Sexuality is the last part that we become enlightened, along with finance. Therapeutic issues often show up in the hesitation created by the yearning to merge and fear for rejection. Here we use sex as a context to talk about emotional health and artfulness. The way you do sex is a reflection of the way you live life. Sexuality is not limited to intercourse, but includes the entire range of sexual relationship: the way you interact with potential mates, the choice of car on a first date — or you just don't care at all. For this article, we will be considering sex as the whole process from flirting to divorcing.

There are times you really need the skills to access the feeling of nothing-matters. One instance is when your art is falling short. No matter how willing you are to give your gift to the world. You can never offer yourself one-hundred percent. As long as you participate, you will always be haunted back by karma, yours and others'. The world's limits and your own limits always ruin the perfection you have achieved through realization. The perpetual feeling of an artist is that you haven't done good enough. When you think your art is the shit, your growth stops. A deep sense of inadequacy is constant. A pianist may have good performances and bad ones, the audience might not even be able to tell, but he knows when he can do better. And chances are that he can always do better. To practice love is to train your body and mind to transmit open space, similar to a pianist training his hands to express music. He does that on a piano; you do that on the world and the woman in your life, which are the same but vary in density. You always feel "Damn it. I could have done better." Therefore it's always good to be able to access the reality that "Nothing matters. This might be a dream." This is spiritual enlightenment.

Circulating energy through sex is one way to cultivate personal power, but not the only. There are enlightened gurus with no flow, yet possessing massive personal power. Their power is based on the consistent recognition of reality's depth, as we have discussed in previous chapters.

Non-ejaculating heart-connected exchange of sexual energy can help you out of depression for real. You will still have good moods and sad moments, but nothing can cause depression anymore. Letting go of the self is part of good sex. For some people, playing the extremes just beyond their neurological limits can help them let go. Just remember to not push on your psyche too far, which is damaged already. Too far of a stretch with red-rope bondage domination flesh scratching plus hot candles dripping in cold tub with Japanese octopus tentacles upside down sixty-nine yelling ex-girlfriend's full name can turn on some, while seriously damage the emotional health of many, even when done with two generally loving hearts. No matter how extreme your sex goes, remain heart connected all the time. Sexual energy stops transmitting the moment heart disconnects. I have been informed by teachers to assign a code word before sexual experiments, a word less used such as umbrella or Madagascar, to stop sex act whenever emotional and causal connection needs to be reestablished, or if someone's psychological dysfunction has been triggered. This way we enact the extremes with love, and carefully watch out for each other's emotional limitations. And Last, don't narrow your attention on body parts or your own pleasure. Don't close your eyes. Go outward, not in. You are creating art together.

34.

One-Side Relationship

_Survive the Breakup of a Close Relationship

T o this point of the book, we have looked at loss and the impermanent nature of arrangements. For the born-masculine people, sexual issue is the biggest distraction knocking them out of the wisdom they have achieved through philosophy. Therefore, there comes a need to address specificity as a reminder in the complication of relationships.

It is not a comfortable topic for men to dwell. Let's get it over with and laugh at whatever unresolved dis-ease left.

The Concept of Relationship Causes Suffering:
Relationship implies the idea of time. The acknowledgment of time is the source of all human suffering. It's illusory for two

people be in any human invented bond in any given moment. A relationship can only seem to exist when future and past are involved. *"In a relationship"* implies your togetherness in near future, the possibility of your further involvement, as well as the past of non-relationship. *"Not in a relationship"* implies that there's no bond of future togetherness. *"No longer in a relationship"* implies the past togetherness and future non-obligation.

Relationship vs. Relating:

The concept of *relationship* can only exist in the structure of time, but *relating* happens in the moment. The more you are empty of concepts, cultural narratives, and the social implications of *relationship*, the more you are free from expectations, and the more you are able to relate in every moment.

Is There a Soulmate?

You can get along with some people more than others. But if you have a strong feeling of *"she is my soulmate."* Chances are that you both have dysfunctions. When her dysfunction complements yours, you feel like she's the soulmate. These dysfunctions are often seeded in your childhood wound.

Seeking Completion vs. Love:

If you feel incomplete without anyone, you can be sure that neediness is taking you over. She might feel valued when you need her, but deep down her trust in you is draining out. It's extremely selfish to go after a woman because you need her.

You are seeing her as a means to fulfill your shitty life. She becomes a role for you to consume. Our society has become dangerously confused between love and neediness. Love needs nothing, but expresses openness and freedom outward. If you aren't dedicated to training yourself in creating warmth in her heart, shut up and go masturbate.

In Order to Recover from a Loss in Relationship, Is There a Place to Utilize the Thinking Mind?

When the accumulated entity of past pain is taking control, the forceful attempt to become present creates conflicts between therapeutic dis-ease and the ease-ful nature of being. Pain and suffering are intensified in this conflict. It's like pulling a spike out of your body. The pulling is the most painful, and then the pain gradually subsides after the pulling. However, sometimes the intense pain during pulling can cause damage. That's when you need to use your thinking mind as a tool. You need to be able to understand the situation in a neutral perspective. Reframe the experience. See the whole picture in order to gain clarity. Then you will flow into the present moment where there are no problems.

How to Turn to Your Friends for Support?

1. Express how you feel without telling story. Do not label, judge, or reconstruct a story out of the actual event. This prevents you from becoming the victim.
2. It's helpful to talk to friends that you have known before or

at the time you met this ex-lover. This reminds you that life has existed before her, and will continue after her.
3. Transmute pain through genuine acceptance. Accept what has already become, and then give your full attention. Learn to appreciate the situation as an impersonal piece of art.
4. Witness. Create space between you and your emotion.

Remember, There Is Always Something More Important:
You have a gift to give, a purpose to fulfill. Every person is brought to the world to offer awareness. Nothing should stop this task. The world is now manifesting temporary distractions to test your capacity to stay on track.

Keep Your Heart Open:
Pain is a bodily response to mental projections. You can feel it in between physical body and emotion. When you are in intense pain, your body try to close down to protect your regarded self. But don't let it. Leave your heart wide open even when it hurts, especially when it hurts. Watch your physical response, feel it thoroughly, taste it and breathe it. Learn to live through your emotions, become it and open as it. Open *as* and *through* the turmoil to who you always are.

Surrender:
Pleasure and pain are inevitable, but suffering is optional. You will suffer whenever you resist what actually is. You might still have hope for the past to have progressed in another way.

When you allow what it has become to be as it is, when you relate with what is directly, rather than relating to an imaginary alternative through the complication of self concern in the head, you find real peace. It is about your relationship with the momentary shape and taste of present situation, instead of with a person which is always subject to further change.

Forgiveness:
Forgiveness starts as letting go. When you accept what the present moment has become completely, without intention to change it, you are ready to forgive what caused it, in you and others.

If people treat you with lie and abandonment, you can be sure that they themselves has been lied to and abandoned this way before. After years of emotional abuse, they become comfortable with this way of dealing with people, and now feels ok to manipulate others this way. They have been victims of your suffering long before you. Once you have compassion to other's torment, you can forgive.

If you have the same level of consciousness and life experience, you will end up choosing the exact same act. If you were her, you would do the same. With understanding comes forgiveness.

Reconnect with Your Masculine Vision:
Once you are in your masculine consciousness, you see the humor in every futile situation.

Even a distraction like reading a gun magazine can help you reconnect with your lower-scale masculine consciousness. And you can go upward from there.

Suffering Is the RESISTANCE of Pain:

Pain is an intrinsic part of life. Suffering is the resistance of pain. If you don't accept pain, holding the belief that it shouldn't be there, you will resist. Resistance creates suffering. When you have a broken leg, you are probably experiencing pain. But you don't have to suffer. Suffering happens only when you resist pain. When you feel a sensation, don't label it, don't judge it, don't hope it to go away, don't call is good or bad, don't give it any value, just let it be a fact. You take note of it, but don't evaluate. Notice your emotional response, but don't evaluate *"why does this happen to me?"* You can have pain while being happy. Happiness starts with acceptance. External events can cause you hurt, but only you can create suffering for yourself. Pain is primary phenomenon, suffering is secondary.

Emotions exist in the phenomenal realm. If you recognize this moment fully, being there with no mental assumption, you won't feel struggle, nor pleasure, but can access peace behind all tension.

Noticing the pain without evaluating is witnessing. It creates space between you and the ego.

Suffering only comes from the opportunistic belief for the past to have gone another way.

Other Reminders to Keep in Mind:

I. Real love never want or fear. Love is free from the desire to possess.

II. Real love can't be diminished. If anything happens that reduces love or even turn it into a blame. That is not love from the start. It may be buried by our selfishness. Then find that part of the relationship that is based on real love. Trust that, and let go of everything else.

III. Allow yourself to free fall.

IV. Instead of wishful thinking, completely destroy the hope for personal good life. Then you are free of tension.

V. Love is the dissolution of ownerships. The ownership of things, people, and most importantly, yourself. Instead of holding onto a separated identity, allow yourself to be lived by the force of truth that's deeper than infatuation.

VI. In this realm, you will never be granted anything permanent. All you can earn from other people is an opportunity to give love.

VII. Relationship is a long-term scenario to practice love. You will never get enough from any arrangement. So give up waiting.

VIII. Let go of everything, and see what's left.

IX. Have no memory. Always see the other person as new.

X. See the other person as an appearing character in your dream. Your character, the room and she are all you. She is a character lit up in your consciousness. She is you.

XI. Even trauma is energy. Don't resist it. Use this energy to motivate you to love, until one day the trauma dissolves.

XII. For everything that you've lost, you got one less thing to lose.

Remember, you are gonna die, she's gonna die, everyone dies in a blink of eye. While find yourself breathing, what else would you rather do than to offer love through the good and bad that appear.

Let's go get a beer.

35.

End the Sense of Lack by Feeling Who You Are

The only way to stop feeling the sense of lack is to dissolve ego. A separated self can never be complete. You will always seek something to make yourself whole, as long as you reflect a self image, as long as you assume yourself to be an isolated individual among a world of other individuals.

By nature you are already whole and complete. You just habitually ignore it and suppress feeling it. To let go of the sense of self is scary, especially after decades of actively trying to strengthen it against other seemingly separated individuals. Thinking is a great capacity to have. But in our tension, thinking is mostly used to improve comfort and security, as well as our perceived value among other individuals who looks like us yet separate from us.

Inevitably, you are present already either you notice it or not yet, otherwise you won't even be here. We tend to reflect our presence by creating a self with a story that has a past and future. In truth, either you reflect your presence or not, you are here as space that is cognizing right now, regardless the activity of your mind and physical body.

That cognizance is who you are and is complete now and always. Anytime you forget, you seek outside. In case you haven't notice, you can never find anything that can fundamentally change the level of your fulfillment for long. Whenever you are knowing and feeling, you *are* this cognizant spaciousness. Everything that you perceive in the appearing world or a dream is contained and arising in this spaciousness. This cognizance is consciousness, who and *where* you are. The only way to feel complete is to be what you are at depth yet above all, which has no sense of self and is inherently at ease.

Chapter 11:
Relate
Beyond Ship

36.

How Much I Love You

The three aspects of love are *Infatuation*, *Sexual Polarity*, and *the Acknowledgment of Mutual Truth*. To love is to be one with. Ideally, we should be loving everything and everyone most of time. It has nothing to do with the other, but purely an ability to access fundamental reality, and then expand that reality to others. Love is to dis-identify with your own thoughts and mind, looking into the other's eyes and knowing who you both are.

By nature we are one with everything. This is not a philo-sophical understanding, but an always accessible feeling. We are granted to think that love happens naturally. This is like to say that the orchestration happens by itself. Without practice, it would have been a discordant drop of glass. Giving love when you are loved is easy. What takes practice is to sustain your loving when absolutely rejected. Both the world and your women will resist your claim in order to test your courage. If you become more aware than the masses, you will very much be disappointed by the world's limits and others' ignorance. Your painting might not be appreciated in your life time, your open heart may hit other's closure. True practice is not to seek love. In case you haven't notice, you will never find the complete loving understanding from anyone. In a life time there might be a few perfect moments that a person feels and understands your most profound heart. Those moments are short-lived and often happen in imagination. To count on those moments is a setup for disappointment. However, you can always give this loving compassion to others in the exact way you wish to receive. The more you have longed for it, the more you know how to offer it. All you can get from anyone is an opportunity to give.

As a man, your total presence is the best gift to a woman. Women are deeply unnoticed for who they truly are. Your complete presence for a few minutes can be a gift she will remember for life. She probably has given up hope on a lot of ideals. Your absolute certainty of the truth that she is light can give strength to her whenever she doubt herself. For us men, is there anything better to do?

Presence is not something you can fake. Your posture and eye contact become gentle and stable when you access pure consciousness. If you are not capable of looking at a coffee cup and love it with the same intensity you would do the love of your life, devoting, contemplating, claiming, then you won't be able to sustain loving when you get absolutely annoyed by your woman, or remain uncollapsed when hurt. This is an art skill you cultivate. You can practice love with everything throughout the day. Success comes and goes; women come and go. This moment remains even though its content changes. Nothing is gained or lost in the openness. Your relationship with this moment and everything it contains is your relationship with the world and your woman.

Love is the nature of everything. It's always there. But we develop shells to protect ourselves from being hurt. That very shell keeps us from the recognition of love.

Romance is what our culture mistakes for love. Infatuation happens on it's own term with little you can do to interfere. We exist in a multidimensional universe. Who the fuck knows why everything is as it is now. A flower doesn't know it is red; a fish doesn't know it is wet. There are influences from other realms that we cannot perceive, such as magnetic field and radio wave. It's often futile to strategize for infatuation, or cease it by force. Sometimes creating space can give infatuation a chance to emerge, or sometimes not.

Even when you have cultivated the capacity to love everyone, you still don't fall in love with everyone. One or two times in our lives and we should be considered lucky. Infatuation is like everything that grows out of nature. Beautiful as it is, it fades away over time.

When romance fades in months or years, what's left for a relationship is the capacity to love, and the capacity to create sexual polarity.

Love is oneness. It's whole. Sexual polarity is to play this oneness in two-bodied form. One body plays the cognizance; the other plays the luminance. At heart we are one. You may love someone deeply without being sexually attracted. To have sexual attraction is to play the masculine and feminine in two bodies.

The masculine is structure and directionality. The feminine is light and energy. In the world of sex, the feminine partner is responsible to provide energy and pleasure; the masculine partner is responsible to provide depth and guidance. Feminine energy is like the ocean, multidirectional yet unanalyzable. The masculine is like a ship, cutting through waves with clarity to get to a vision.

When the masculine consciousness is trustable, the feminine partner can relax into her jellyfish nature, without having to think where to go. She is trusting the masculine aligning force.

Masculinity is ultimately consciousness. Feminine radiance is ultimately light. Your relationship with this moment is your relationship with your woman, because the nature of this moment's appearance is a woman. A *moment* has to have both cognizance and luminance. Cognizance claims to know for absolute, with authentic certainty and no fear of inconclusion. Luminance desires to show her form inside out. Human awareness is cognizing in every instant of experience. The training for a man is to be transparent to this outside-in cognizance.

Your capacity to cognize reflects your level of consciousness. Consciousness is the Masculine.

Romance comes and goes. When it fades, you are left with the capacity to give love, and the skillfulness to paint polarity.

37.

Three Steps of Relating

Presence is whole. It's both consciousness and light. You can be present as consciousness or present as light. To form polarity, you need one partner to incarnate consciousness, while the other incarnates light.

Being present should be a spontaneous endeavor rather than a forceful constipation. The practice is to be present in all situations regardless of the content of this moment. The practicality is to lay out life in ways that have you slip into presence every time you wake up. It's not always a realistic thing to do, and therefore you also need to learn the art of being present regardless of where you are. After that you can use the refinement to offer this presence, as it can embody both the content of this moment and the background of it. Chances are that once you are present in the now, you will naturally reside into either masculine presence or feminine presence.

Three Steps of Relating:
The first step is to be in your body, which means to recognize presence within you. Presence is whole of both consciousness and light. You should simply feel at ease in your own body. Relaxed.

The second step is to recognize the same presence in the other. This is the act to relate. Relating is to recognize yourself in the other as if you are one. The nature of you is consciousness and light. By recognizing presence in your body, you are being the nature of yourself. This self is not confined by appearing bodies. Therefore once you are present in your body as consciousness and light, you are ready to recognize the same one presence in the other. This is how you relate to another being. Be it a cat a human or a tree.

The third step is to form polarity. Polarity can only be created on top of connection. Connection is established by recognizing presence in your body and seeing the same presence in the other. However, relating by itself is not necessarily sexy. Polarity happens when one person is as consciousness and the other person is as light, while staying related as one presence.

How to Relate in Polarity?
Presence is whole. It's the nature of you and I and all humans. Everything that has the capacity to know and feel is spacious consciousness; everything that shows is luminance. As human beings, we are both. We can cognize and witness, as well as be seen as appearing forms. By nature, we are whole beings.

But in order to create polarity – though we can choose not to – you have to reside in one side and have someone reside into the other. While you are present in your body relating with your partner as one presence, gradually shift the quality of your presence, from whole of consciousness and light towards consciousness only. While maintaining the connection established, you are present as consciousness that knows and feels. You are the unchanging spaciousness where all luminance is lit up. While you shift into pure cognizance, your partner resides into luminance, being present as light that shows and moves.

Connection is never lost. You both are still one presence, one as consciousness recognizing the other as light presence, one as light trusting the other as God presence.

From Connection to Polarity:

Before you create polarity, connection has to be established. To relate is to recognize yourself as the other. By nature you *are* the other and everything else. All you need to do is to re-remember who you are. All of us are consciousness and luminance both. By being present in your body, you access your true nature. Then the realization that you are also as everything and everyone then comes naturally.

This is for the sake of relating with another human or another thing. Being in your body, recognize presence in you, and then recognize the same presence in the other.

Stopping here is totally fine. But if you want to create the passion of sexual re-tie-back, the next level is to reside into consciousness or light, as your partner resides into the other. Consciousness and light are one to begin with. By taking them apart in two bodies, the urge to re-unite as one is created. While connection of presence is maintained, the further consciousness and light are apart, the more intense the force of reunion is. This is the cause of sexual passion.

Applications and Practice:
The decision is how you want to relate with the other. You can relate to objects and things and animals and women by recognizing the same one presence, or further by residing into consciousness recognizing the other as light presence. You can relate with your men friends through mutual recognition of one neutral presence, or better both as consciousness in polarity with the appearing world – *"Dude, check out those chicks"*, for instance. In times of potential conflict, you can reside into pure witnessing consciousness that can't be disturbed, feeling and breathing with your adrenaline-rushed opponent. This witness state of not running not grasping – being there with total presence – immediately put you in to an extremely masculine disposition.

You can practice all three of presence, relating, and polarity with anything anywhere if you are a man who's identified with masculine consciousness. If you are more identified with feminine energy, you can still practice relating as presence with everything. Yet if you are to reside into light presence, you can only practice polarity with cognizant beings – masculine identified human or an imagined perfect man, since objects are by nature luminance with no capacity to perceive, and therefore no capacity to play consciousness.

Anytime you practice deep relating. It's always easier to practice relating with an object, an animal, or a wall. To relate with humans can be more difficult, for our social face and shells developed to protect our separated identity. We often worry about how people think of us and therefore recoil. To be present in your body in front of a human can be more obstructed than of a wall or a flower, because you won't be afraid of accidentally offending a wall. It's a good practice to train to relate with things before you can do well with humans.

In Summary, This Is How to Relate to Another Anything:
1. Be in your body. Recognize presence in you. Presence is whole. Whole is consciousness plus light.
2. Relate. Recognize presence in the other. Be as the same one presence with the other.
3. Relate in polarity. Reside into the Masculine aspect, while maintaining established connection of the one presence. As consciousness, let go of light. Consciousness knows, feels, is space, is the witness.

38.

Three Levels of Connection in Practice

Real connection exists on all three levels of causal, subtle and gross. Although a good moment often happens without our intervention, here are some guidelines to help you replicate the experience of boundaryless communion.

First Is to Connect Causally (Not Casually):
• Feel the part of you that is there before you were born or as young as you can remember. Feel the part of the other person that is there before she was born. And then combine the two.
• Feel that this is a dream that you are in. Someone is watching all of you. When you look into the other's eyes you see yourself, because it is a dream. Both you and the other are the one that is dreaming.

Then Connect on the Subtle Level:

- Synchronize breathing with her.
- Breathe her quality. She has a vibratory flavor that you can combine with. Breathe her in.
- Occupy her body. Wear her shape, posture and movement.

The Last Is Gross-Level Connection:

- A dance or a walk. You merge in physical activity with the other person.

39.

Ah... Life

_What's Out There Beyond Physical Bodies

*Contemplate life as if you are listening to the beauty
of meaningless ocean. You will get caught up in complication whenever you believe the sound of waves is
trying to tell you something. It's not. Just listen.*

P eople have been talking way too much about how you
should live your life. But it is actually very simple one
thing to do. That is to deal with everything as energy.
Energy comes through external forms. Forms appear to be
separate, and so we have been taught to deal with people, self,
and environment.

But there's nothing you can do with physical forms. Communication in words is only a resulting scene projected from what
you have been dealing with – the constantly reforming energetic
composition showing up as seemingly solid individuals. When

you are talking to a friend, you are dealing with the emotion that come through the form of that friend. Appearing that your vocal chord is vibrating syllables in response to your friend's facial muscle tension, you are in deed taming the emotional energy. This realization alone, simplifies most of our social obstacles.

Forms are worthless. If a person dies, he is gone. His body may still represents the memories of him. But the person is not in the body anymore. It's quite clear that when you were interacting with this person, you were dealing with that part of him that is now gone. That part of him existed in the subtle realm which includes mental realm and emotional realm.

Every person has three entities of being. The physical entity, the subtle entity, and the causal entity. Physical entity is what you see, a human, fat or skinny, male or female. The subtle entity is less condensed than the physical body, to a point that we can't see. It includes the patterns of thoughts and emotions, the internal neurological shape, the masculine or feminine qualities. Subtle bodies and physical bodies all die. Perhaps subtle entity can continue after death, but the physical body certainly dies as it rots. Causal body is… is a wrong name to start with, because there's no body at all. Subtle entity is still something that is here – even though we can't see an emotion or a thought. It is subject to be felt as *something* unsayable. However, when it comes to the causal level, there's only an empty, colorless, size-less, quality-less …open AH. It's not exactly space because space is still something to be comprehended by the mind. Causality is an empty AH-ness. The chanting sound *"Om"* is a completion sound of the universe from beginning to end. The sound starts with *"Ah"* and ends with mouth closed. AH is the origin of universe, the no-thing place of open space.

You are never in friendship with physical bodies. That's why when someone dies, his body is no longer felt as him. What's missing is the subtle entity of him. That subtle body has departed from physical form, and you can no longer experience it through this form. He might still be out there in some other realms.

If you can see through the less-condensed form of subtle body, to the causal AH-like openness, which is him most fundamentally, you can't lose him. Who you are at beginning is this same open AH. You are him, everything is everybody. It is not a mental masturbation. It is what the word *"truth"* was invented to describe. You can lose physical bodies of people you love, but the subtle interaction doesn't need forms to be at the same location. Long-distance lovers know this. Eventually, you lose the subtle body of everyone. Maybe it's continued somewhere, or even some other realms or life times. But you'll still part ways in the end. What you can never lose is the AH of openness that is nowhere and everywhere.

Love is eternal. This is what they meant. The only love that can't be torn apart is the love that's free from time and form.

40.

Cultivate Relationship with Everyone's Mind

Love wants to come through, and therefore it ripples as forms. Space knows and feels. It witnesses and beholds these ripples. Consciousness can always see love through appearances. As consciousness sees the love that is in everything, your appearing self is rising together with all appearing selves.

As consciousness, you are free to develop a relationship with the mind. Your mind will be your companion in this human experience most time that you are awake. Mind is in the realm of manifestation. All forms of manifestation are a blended one. Therefore your mind is also everyone's mind. Of course they appear to be separate.

Next time when you are with another person, you can use the same relationship that you have been cultivating with your own mind. Relate consciousness with the other's mind just like you do with your own. In this way you are no longer attending to your own thoughts, but putting attention onto her feelings. No matter how short you come to know each other, the relationship has been there for as long as you are with your mind. The same relationship, with the same essence in form of a different mind. They are the same one, really.

Chapter 12:
See Time in Space

41.

As Blob Hits Ocean Floor, We Feel Time (Part I)

E nlightenment is about feeling the fundamental truth. As life becomes more complex, seeing through drama to the basic silence becomes the practice.

To talk about how we came from fundamental perception to a complex identification, let's start with the evolution process.

In the beginning, creatures exist in the ocean. As we know that if you drop oil into water, it becomes round. Water offers equal pressure from all directions to whatever is merged in it. In the case of these prehistorical creatures, which have similar density to sea water, they float in the middle of the ocean, instead of coming onto the surface like oil in water. However just like how water shapes the oil drop, ocean shaped those early creatures into spherical round blobs.

For the blobs, there is no distinction of up and down, left and right, front and back. The sensors are evenly distributed over its surface. It feels towards all directions.

Gradually, one of the blobs sank to the ocean floor. It is still round, but now has a bottom. This is when the species develops distinction between up and down.

Then these round blobs with flat bottom were moved by the current to a certain direction. Through evolution, those who had sense organs developed on one side gained survival advantage, because they can now see what's in front and where it's going. Over time, the sensory capacity of early animals migrates to one side. They now have not just top and bottom, but also front and back.

This stage lasted for a long time in evolution, since being able to tell where ground is and where it's going is more than sufficient for most animals' survival needs.

Until those sea creatures evolved into humans. We start to distinguish left and right. For most animals today, all they need are legs on the bottom that can run on the earth, and eyes that see where they're going. Only human and very few species have developed the ability to tell left and right.

As humans that have gone a long way in evolution, we have a sense of up and down, front and back , as well as left and right. However because the distinction of up-down was developed earlier than the rest, it carries more emotional tone.

If someone yell at you *"Get down!"*, it feels more urgent and determined than *"Get left!"* Because humans were evolved from sea creatures that came up to the surface following the light above water, upward-ness feels like hope and higher domain. The emotional flavor of up-ness is heaven and light. This hint is subtle yet profound. If you try to close your eyes and face up to the sky, it feels different emotionally than you looking down with eyes shut. Throughout the world, up-ness represents something more permanent than down. What's up there is less subject to change, yet down is full of complex entanglement. Whenever we feel trapped in this world's drama, we look up with a subtle feeling of *"Get me out of this madness."*

Throughout our lives, we rarely get confused with up and down, or left and right. However, we do sometimes say *"turn left"* when we meant right. If you are sitting with someone face to face, it may take you half a second to tell which eye is your partner's left eye. If you recall your childhood learning experience, you probably learned up-down and front-back years before left-right.

Confusion of left-right is even regarded as a lack of intelligence. It is a distinction we have just started to develop.

As humans, our top and bottom look nothing alike. Our front and back look pretty different. But our left and right... They are almost identical.

The evolution of distinction between left and right has just started. Most of us has a heart on the left side in the chest, with exceptions. Some people are right-handed while others are lefties. Many people have very slight difference between a left eye and right eye, or the shape of their ears. Compare to how far we have distinguished up-and-down, front-and-back, those differences are tiny. But this is the coming step of evolution, as it has started.

This step can progress really fast with the help of technological advance. We may soon develop the right hand for writing and left hand for typing as we put on artificial limbs as extensions of hands not too far from now.

With the development of awareness in these directions, we come to experience the three-dimensional space. Up-down, front-back, left-right.

We might want to be reminded that many creatures are still living in a two-dimensional or one-dimensional world. There are still blobs in the ocean. Left and right mean nothing to a jelly fish. An ant's world is what's directly in front of it. Can you imagine what it would be like to be an earthworm?

We might feel overly fortunate that we can experience more than an earthworm. But what if there are even more dimensions that we are not yet capable of comprehending?

In deed, there is the next dimension of time. Although an ant isn't able to experience left-right, left and right do exist for an ant. If it turned to the wrong direction, it won't get back to its colony. They need to have a communication in their own methods. But the ant won't be able to understand that it turned left while should have turned right, like humans can say. They are in the reality of left-right, and yet not able to experience it directly. Similarly, we humans live in the reality of time, and yet not able to experience time directly. We need devices to indicate this dimension – we wear watches. Imagine an ant wears a device to remind itself the existence of left-right. This is how under-developed we are in comprehension of time. Past-and-future is as real as left-right to an ant. We do grow old over time, which we can't perceive in the moment.

Even though the awareness of left and right was later-developed, we already have a good grasp of it. Everything in three-dimension space, we can comprehend.

Let's take a look at the dimension of time then, What is in this dimension?

The answer: change.

We can see the result of change, but we can't see change itself with the same comprehension as we can a spoon in space. Change causes the spoon in three dimension to deteriorate. But change itself happens beyond the three dimensions which we are able to distinguish. An ant experiences the result of left-right, but can't feel the difference. We experience the result of time, but have never experienced time.

When a blob doesn't have a bottom, it doesn't know there's up-and-down. It may sense gravitational pull, but merely as a force. It's unaware of it's own potential to develop a bottom, letting alone to transform into a human billions of years later.

Hitting the ocean floor triggers the development of up-down. Being moved by current leads to the distinction of front-back. Now a few billion years later, we are aware that there's something called time dimension. Does it mean that our existing bodies will be transformed once we touch something that can only be seen in the forth dimension, just as the first blob hitting ocean floor started to develop in the up-down reality?

What is it that we can hit in time?

For a blob that doesn't know up-and-down, gravity is something that it can sense but not zero-dimensionize. All it can be aware of is the dimensionless feeling from all around it. The first dimension's influence is felt, and yet not understood in its reality.

It is very much like the way we experience time as humans.

Imagine the instant when blob touches ground. The ground is not felt as an end of downward. But as a sensation in zero-dimension awareness. The concept of downwardness comes long after the first touch. The development of awareness and bodily change come when the sensation of flat supporting force from floor becomes part of constancy. Before the blob acknowledges the first dimension, it has been feeling the floor with panoramic spread-out zero-dimension consciousness for a long period.

Remember, it all starts with hitting something that exists in up-and-down dimension.

To evolve into a forth-dimension species, humans must sense what is in the forth dimension, with our three-dimensional awareness. And as this sensation of whatever in forth dimension becomes a constancy, we will begin to acknowledge this dimension and develop a direct awareness of time. Not just experiencing time through its effect in three-dimensional world, but to be able to move through it, just like you can move forward and back, turn left and right.

We can feel the influence of change with three-dimension awareness, just like a blob can feel the result of gravity with zero-dimension all-around senses. Now we just need to *"hit the ground"*.

Ground exists in one dimension of up-and-down. What exists in the forth dimension of time?

Once again it's change.

Now what we need to do is to feel change as an *object* in space. For humans to feel forth-dimension existence with three-dimensional awareness is just like the blob feeling one-dimensional existence with pre-dimentional cognizance.

What are the subjects beyond three-dimensional space?

One of them is emotion. Emotions can't exist without time. It moves like ocean waves. If you slice that wave vertically and take out that slice. You get a motionless straight line. Emotion can only come to existence with reference to past and future.

Complete presence in the now is emotionless. Imagine you have some strange type of memory loss — every half second you lose all memories of the past. You will never know your name, where you are, or whom you are acquainted with. And you will never have emotions, either good or bad ones. Just as you start to be amused, you forget the subject you are about to laugh at. Just as you start to get irritated, you forget what is bothering you. Your life is completely new and awe-some in every moment. You're being reborn in every half second. We'll come back to it later. But for now, we notice that such a person won't have emotions.

Emotion necessitates change in continuity of time. It is an result of time dimension, just like ocean floor is an result of up-down dimension. As a floating blob felt gravity from ground, we can feel emotion from something we haven't conceptualized as *"ground"* or *"ocean floor"* yet.

Now, to advance our development in time dimension, we can start by feeling emotion as an *object* in space, with our well-developed three-dimension awareness. See the change in emotions as an existing *object* in space, without going through time.

Now we are ready to introduce the ant on the ruler.

If we put an ant on a ruler, it doesn't know what it is on. The ruler for this ant is an surface extended in front of it, with marks of distance. It starts to run along the length of ruler. As it approaches the end, it craws to the back side of the ruler. The ant will craw all around the ruler back to where it started, and maybe take a few runs to the side of the ruler. The reality of ruler is being unfolded inch by inch, in time. After a while, the ant learned that it's a ruler.

But for humans, we can tell instantly that it is a ruler, without any time. We don't need to run our noses along the length over centimeter marks for five minutes to conclude that it's a ruler. It's obvious in *space*, once you have the ability to see all three dimensions. However, the ant's reality is right in front of it. The truth of ruler has to be revealed *over time* for the ant.

We might feel superior over the ignorance of ants. But wait. We're not that more advanced than ants. There are only three dimensions that we are able to move within at will and comprehend directly without the reference of results from motion. We still need time to unfold our life's story. One centimeter at a time, for quite a while.

The practice towards forth-dimension awareness involves seeing the whole ruler-length of your life all *at once*, from birth to childhood to first kiss to adult life to the graveyard, as an *object* in space, without time to unfold.

For the ant, its experience is changing as it runs along the ruler. One centimeter, two centimeter, three centimeter, an edge, another side, once inch, two inch...

For us humans, our experience is changing as we run along the journey. One day, another day, another day, marriage, another side, one year, another year, another year...

It must be quite a promising exploration for that ant, just like we are having fun exploring another day.

While you discover the ruler over time, someone that sees it as a ruler is laughing at the whole thing. *It's a fucking ruler, dude.* Either on a ruler or a journey, change happens in time. For every centimeter there's a different number. You will stay interested until you see the whole changing of numbers, or the whole changing of emotions, as something floating in space instead of unfolding in time.

This step of advance is to see change that can only exist in time as an *object* that we can perceive instantly with three-dimensional awareness.

When the blob was pulled by gravity, it had no choice to go back up. Only after it has developed up-and-down features

—fins or tentacles, can they swim up. When human is pulled to go through time, we don't have choice to go backwards. Unless we develop a past-and-future feature someday, biologically or technologically.

The beginning of developing a bottom was to feel one dimension existence with pre-dimensional cognizant capacity.

The beginning of developing anything in the dimension of time, is to feel time-dimension existence of change with three-dimensional cognition. Once you can see the whole process of changing drama all at once, you will be free to choose to run along the ruler or not. You've already seen the whole damn thing, the rest is for the fun of it.

This evolution of comprehension and physical forms is endless. It must have been pretty abstract for the blob to experience time at all. After time-dimension, who knows what else is next.

Remember back in the day when we can't even tell up and down? As cute little blobs of course. Now we are driving a car with a phone telling us to turn left and a directory to tell us to go up to the 20th floor and walk to the end of hall way.

Imagine few thousand years from now, a device is going to tell you to turn past, go forward for two miles, and then turn past again at a 60 degree angle… We can't comprehend what is going to be.

To be continued…

42.

As Blob Hits Ocean Floor, We Feel Time (Part II)

Enlightenment is about realizing the fundamental of existence, not to develop more complexity.

Remember when you were a blob, you were peaceful and full of joy every single day, even though you had no idea what a day is. May just be because of the knowledge of what a day is, that you stopped being joyful. Time is the source of our suffering as humans.

For a blob that has just hit the floor, forward is the source of its fearful tension, as it is pushed forward by water, and yet hasn't developed eyes to see what's ahead, or legs to move on its own will. Forward has influenced its life, but it weren't able to control or even know what forward is.

Life's change affects all humans. We are pushed to a direction we call future, and yet have not developed the bodily function to move backwards. We don't even have the sensory organ to see what's ahead in the future.

The blob was pushed into the forward. Humans are pushed into the future. Until we see the whole ruler, we stay bewildered.

As our capacity on the axle of left and right evolves, some sensitive humans begin to sense change in the time axle. You might have visited a place and suddenly realized that you have dreamed of this place before. You might have had an unexplainable negative feeling about an event in the future and something bad did happen as the event approached. You might have had sudden shocks of Deja Vu. In a partnership went to train wreck, you might have felt it in the instant of beginning. This can be regarded as the very first sign of sensory development in time axle.

As the blobs were moved forward, sensors migrate to the front over generations. Those who trusted the intuitive response from the frontal sensors can react and adapt to the terrain. They had more chances to survive and replicate. This is before eyes are developed, right in the beginning stage of sensors moving to one side.

We humans talk about trusting intuition and gut-feelings. We don't know for sure, but maybe there are sensors that have started to develop right in your gut. Scientists now found out that our gut has its own nervous system. It functions like an independent brain with neurons. Some people realized that fixing digestion can solve depression and anxiety. Throughout the world, cultures have expressions of "trusting your gut" and "following you heart" in various languages. We don't say "trusting your Adam's apple" or "following your elbow".

We really can't know what will be developed in tens of thousands of years. Blobs that trusted their intuitive sensors on the font survived and evolved, while those whose front senses were less developed were wiped out of gene pool or stayed as blobs.

Maybe one day we'll develop "eyes" that can feel future and "legs" that can run back in time. However, none of this will alleviate our suffering and fear. Forward was blob's source of suffering, as time is ours. The suffering of forward forces blobs to evolve eyes. The suffering of time forces us to trust intuition. Adapt or die.

Once you comprehend a new dimension, the next one gives you the equal amount of suffering. This is the realm of expansion originated from the Big Bang. The universe is expanding in complexity. Even our civilization in the past few decades has become significantly more complex.

On a larger scale, creatures evolve and become aware of more and more dimensions, from up-and-down to front-back left-right, and even close to future-and-past.

Developing comprehension of the next dimension might be good for survival, but not necessarily for enlightenment. In fact, nothing you do just for the sake of enlightenment is directly beneficent for the survival of gene. Look at Ramana Maharshi or Gandhi, they are not trillionaires having sex with different fertile women whole day. Yet unenlightened dictators are.

That being said, sages rise above suffering. Dictators don't.

Enlightenment in the original sense is reducing complexity to the basic nature of existence. Before the Big Bang, it was perfect peace, absolute enlightenment. It was as the dance of universe starts, that the complexity spreads and ties knots.

Scientists predict that there will be a contraction through which our universe will come back to the origin state of nothing.

I look around and imagine that space is a dude sitting in the living room by himself. Suddenly he becomes really bored and gets up dancing. He throws pillow around and sings high notes. After a while he finds himself a retard. So he sits down again back to the prehistorical peace.

It is this place, as bizarre as it sounds. We're in a dude's living room listening to him hitting hight notes and being thrown around as pillows.

The room's getting more and more of a mess. Now we, as pillows, are evolved at the beginning of experiencing time.

We are bewildered by the future, as ants are confused by left and right, as blobs are threatened by forward. The only way out of suffering happens to be the only way to evolve, happens to be the way of enlightenment.

For a blob to adapt to terrains. It has to use the panoramic sensors developed when it was floating. The non-differentiated sensory ability as a single point in zero-dimension must be utilized to feel the *forward*. The unknown support from ocean floor, as in up-down existence, has to be comprehended as water pressure experienced with evenly distributed sensors.

For humans to adapt to the change in time, we have to utilize our developed awareness of space. We have to use our capacity to see object in space to approach *change*. Emotions and relationships can only exist in the reality of *change*. They can't be felt without time or *change* that happens in time, as the patient who loses memory every half-second will have no emotions or relationships. We see him as misfortunate, but the way he lives life might just be the key to free you from private torments.

The key here is to be free from time. Be the human that can see the ruler in space, instead of the ant that has to discover it in time.

Only in this case, the ruler is called life. It's tempting to start running along and never stop. When you take this capacity of feeling object into the realm of emotions and relationships, you can be free from the drama of counting centimeters. Your obsessions are loosened as you see the obviousness. Until one day our capacity of experiencing time is developed, the best we can do is to feel comprehensively, to see the time-dimension existence in space. This is the practice for evolution.

Feelings, emotions, life situations. We see everything in our life past-and-future all at once, rising in space solidified into a whole object that is obviously is, without need for time.

Eventually, we can take this fundamental perception all the way back to zero-dimension. We can feel as if surrounded by water. Every cell of our skin becomes alive again. We feel air's movement with neck and face, the pressure from fabrics resting on the legs and warmth in the layers of our shirts and jackets. You become a tender organism that can feel outward in all directions with equal sensitivity. You forget about past and future, up and down. It all becomes a blur in the feeling solidity of the pre-dimensional *now*. Maybe, this is utter enlightenment, the fundamental joy of being. To feel everything like a blob would, undifferentiated, free from concept, without judgment.

The expansion of Big Bang brings prosperity. The contraction of matter leads to peace's no thing. We don't know what's going to happen. But they can happen all together, as a solid entirety for a instant.

43.

Listen
with Your Whole Body

We will be looking at music and the development of awareness. What we call external are objects we can perceive in space. Our sensory awareness has developed through a period of evolution to perceive the three-dimensional world directly.

However there are more dimensions than up-down, front-back, left-right. The next dimension that we might develop to be in direct contact with is the forth dimension of time. Humans experience time indirectly through the result of whatever exist in time. We see the result of change but not change itself.

Things that we can't perceive in space, we call them internal. Emotions and moods are internal. Those internal things are subjective instead of objective. In other words, we can't point to an emotion. We can point at a car a table a spoon. But not an anger, a comfort, a fear, or an affection. And those internal subjects are simply what our nervous system yet able to objectify. Our perception only comprehend what's in the three dimension space. Whatever beyond exists in time. So-called internal emotions are simply our experience of time. Or more precisely, the experience of emotion is the experience of the result of change in time.

Internal feelings exist in time. Without reference and flow in time, an emotion can't stand on a single point of present moment. To feel emotion is to feel internality as external objects, seeing it in space, without the need for time to unfold. To develop sensitivity is to grow the capacity to see what is usually experienced in time as an object in space, perceiving the result of movement in time as a whole that is all at once.

We as a species will evolve to poke more dimensions with sensory ability. We came from blobs floating in ocean, sinking to the ocean floor forming a bottom, and then we gradually come to understand front-back, left-right. We develop our bodies according to our ability to distinct. Our head looks very deferent than legs, front looks quite different than the back, and we even start to evolve as left-handed or right-handed as our left ear might look slightly different than the right. Meanwhile, we are starting to have the capacity of seeing what's in time. We are at the starting point in evolution where we begin to sense the current that encompasses past and future.

If wind can be dyed with color, you will be able to see it. Then as it's approaching a tree, you can predict that "the leaves on that tree is going to fall in ten seconds". People who can't see the color of wind will think you are predicting future. But all you did is being able to perceive more. Once you see color of the wind, you see how the wind moves and how it's going to blow through the branches, and therefore "predict" how the leaves will react to the wind.

The reason we can't know future is firstly because we can't perceive what is in time. On the level of intellect, we understand that change exists in time, beyond a single point of momentary reality of three-dimensional space. Therefore to develop any capacity in time dimension is to grow the ability to see change. For now, we only have three distinctions. And therefore, our approach to perceiving change has to be the objectification of the *process of change*. Not just the result, but the less noticeable process. We need to cultivate this time-dimension awareness by practicing objectifying emotions and the gradual yet constant change in all relations. To see an emotion in time as an object right now that rises up in space, without the need to walk through it in time. It's helpful to point out that this objectification is done by perception in the moment, not a secondary interpretation or labeling. Once it has been labeled, it becomes a mental model, which is not what the objectified emotion actually is.

Music is something that exists only in time. Take any piece of music, you have to listen to it in time. Unlike a painting, which you can see in an instant. Music is the artistically arranged change of tension-and-release unfolding through time. If you play a song for 0.00001 second, you can't perceive it. But if you play for even ten seconds, you start to feel its emotional quality. If we examine a single note, we find that a note is a vibrational frequency. This frequency has to be expressed in time, even though it can be represented on a graph in space. The difference between a high note and a lower note lies in the frequency of vibration. Vibration is motion, which means that it can't happen without change in time. Without change and the dimension of time, a vibration will freeze at one single frame. Therefore we can't even call it vibration anymore. To play any note, time is necessitated.

Because of the vibratory nature, to perceive a note is to perceive the result of change in time. Distinguishing notes means knowing vibrational qualities that happen in time dimension. If your awareness is developed to tell which note was played, you are capable of objectifying qualities of vibration that is usually experienced in time.

Therefore, the development of musical awareness, is the development of perception of time, and is the development of internal sensitivity. This is why we find musicians often more intact with emotions and energetic flow. They are more advanced in perceiving what's internal, what's in time than most people.

To tell what note is played, the training is to see it as color. A musician with perfect pitch is often trained to perceive notes by its visual quality, to see a note in space, being able to tell what it is instantly. This is the way to objectify vibration in time. See a note's flavor as an object in space and then you are able to tell its shape.

DJs often have cultivated emotional awareness of the crowd. A good DJ is aware where the audience's energy is at as if the audience is a qualitative entity, and at same time possesses an inventory of musical vibrational "colors" that can take the qualitative entity of crowd to the next variational frequency. In a sense, he is not dealing with people and music, but qualities, colors. A DJ sees what's auditory to most people as visions. He is working like a painter calibrating harmony, conflict and progression of color in form of music, which has to be experienced in time by the masses. What makes a DJ cool is awareness, and this awareness comes from the perception of musical energy in space, as qualities, instantly.

Here's the subject of our development: the awareness of sound. Perhaps with musical notes, songs, as well as sound waves throughout the day. Eventually, this expands to the art of spacious listening.

Unlike visual perception, listening necessitates the time dimension. A sound can't be made without time for the wave to vibrate. Therefore, the awareness of sound becomes the awareness of forth dimension. You perceive what's in time as an object in space.

Next time when you are listening to your girlfriend, instead of grasping on the content of words, listen to it like ocean waves. The wave has energetic qualities, but doesn't have any meaning. Our communications happen mostly on the subtle level. While words transmit information, how a person deliver the words is involuntarily reflecting a subtle transmission of aggression or blessing. When we can listen not just with our ears, but with every cell of our body, when we are aware of the energetic disposition behind words, we are truly listening. This act of listening makes you perceive words as a piece of melodic notes, as a painting of art in space. It's there as a whole, of which you can tell quality instantly, with perception in space, not exploration through time.

When you are aware of people's expression as a whole solid entity of qualities, you are aware of what is in time. The unfolding of this art piece continues as the person delivers words. But you see the whole thing without need to wait and discover where it goes. With an alert awareness, you already know where the conversation's gonna turn into as it begins. You already know if a relationship is going to work or not as you meet a person.

This ability of seeing and objectifying puts you into a spacial awareness not just of three dimensions but of future and past as an entirety. Widened awareness is consciousness. It is the primordial unmanifested background. Residing into this background, you manifest words and actions with spontaneity.

44.

To the Other Side of the Glass Wall

A fly wants to get into a room, hitting its head on the glass wall. The glass remains unseen, and the fly won't know that the only way in is through the window next to the wall. It will keep banging head against the invisible barrier, or incidentally find the opening.

A tube is tied into a knot. An ant is in the tube. It crawls inside the knot and bites through the tube, one wall after another. The ant will not see the entire knot, or the unnecessity of biting through walls.

The ant's life is limited by the shape of knot. As it burrows through walls or crawls inside the tunnel, the shape of knot is an entire formation of object that is already tied. Free will is only a variety of ways to burrow through a knotted fate in space.

S top waiting. It doesn't mean to act with the flow of appearance that includes your thoughts, emotions, life situations, but to stop waiting to see the entire current. Time becomes spacious. Past-present-future, they all rise simultaneously as a whole. It's going nowhere, but an object in space that has already happened.

You might never be able to see the current as apparent as a window on a glass wall. But you can feel where the current is moving you to, when you feel its entirety.

Move as this entirety wants to move you. It's the only way you can go anywhere at all. It might take you into the window, or take you away from the glass wall, or it might not want you to move for now. But at least, you won't be busting your head. Your glass wall is the wait for something or someone in time.

By recognizing this entire current as a whole arising in space without need for time to unfold, you loosen the obsession with the other side. The fly realizes its futility on the invisible barrier.

There might be no window at all. You can't see for sure. All you can do is to feel the current as deeply as you can, and allow it to move through you.

So do you try to get in the room?
You must be aware that there might be no window at all. You might never be able to get in. Even if there is a window, the chance of finding the window by hitting with your head repeatedly is very slim. It's like looking for a keychain in the dark, very disorienting.

The knot is there. You can drill through the shell of the tube, or crawl over the surface. Its shape is already as it has become, but how you go through it is uncertain. Either way, you aren't able to see how the knot is tied. The object-like nature of the current can only be felt in the free fall of awareness.

How can you find the window then?
First, stop hitting on glass wall.

Then, feel the current. If you are going to move anywhere at all, you will be moved by the current. The appearing flow is just an expression of the current. Going with flow is getting lost in chaos. You need to go with the deeper current instead. If the current doesn't want to move you, don't move. Keep practicing feeling it. It will move you sooner or later. Again, do not believe the appearing fluctuation, but only trust the deeper current.

One skill essential is to surf on the appearance. What the current moves you into might or might not be where the appearing flow is going. On the one hand you feel the current; on the other hand you develop the capacity to sail through the appearing fluctuation. You can't direct the entirety of current at will, just like an ant won't be able to redesign the knot. But you can surf its expression, the appearances which are your thoughts, emotions, life situations.

What if you have developed the skill to surf, but are not willing to go with the current?

You will be able to navigate through the appearing flow fast, experimenting routes that might lead into the room, hitting the glass over and over again, until you find the window, or never find the window.

Is the current always leading you to the window, if there is one? If there is a window, it means that it's a part of the whole already, waiting to be unfolded to you. How soon it will be unfolded to you depends on:

- how complex the knot – or entirety – is,
- how active the movement of current is,
- and how fast you can move along when the wind is actively blowing.

The complexity of knot is your karma. It is tied this way by the momentum of billions of years of genetic traits – your ancestors' insecurity and lust, your culture's collective evolution, your family situation, your early sexual experiences, as well as you own decisions as an adult. If you can be free from all karma, the knot will disappear. Then you can do anything.

The way out of karma is through the absent of concept. However, even though we can become free from concepts in this moment, the involvement in a world in time often necessitates roles and predetermined relations. After all, we have to eat, and that perpetuates the karma of bodily existence, which carries psychological existence and eventually social existence.

Therefore, genetic karma, neurological karma, psychological karma, social karma, relational karma often find ways to haunt you back through a world of concepts.

Besides the shape of karma, whether the current will lead you into the window also depends on the force of wind and you own ability to harvest the wind. You have to follow the current to go anywhere at all. The current is the unfolding process of the entirety that is already built in space as a whole object. Where an ant can possibly crawl to, depends on the shape of the object – the knot you can't see when you are in or on it. The only thing you can do besides feeling the current is to cultivate the capacity to sail faster when the current is moving you. That capacity is to navigate through appearances, riding the surface wave, maximizing the advantage of the current's force. If there is a window, and you are moving faster enough, you are going to encounter the window down the line. Meanwhile, be aware that there might be just a bland wall with no window.

It's equally important to *feel* the current underneath appearing happenings, and to cultivate the capacity to *ride* a superficial wave. The deeper current often expresses as a fluctuating situation. You have a choice to ride it, float with it, be distracted by it or even drown in it. The current will be pushing you for a limited while, and then subside or change direction. Even the most favorable current won't be able to help, until you are able to ride its waves. Be still, be capable, and pay attention to silence. The ocean will unfold its entirety for you.

Are you going to have another window if you miss it?
It will not be the same window. Your experience is unfolding in time. It doesn't go backwards.

Let's not even use window as a metaphor for a second. You're surrounded by glass walls. Only in the direction that the current moves you towards, is there no obstruction of walls. That's how the current can be funneled to the opening of possibility. In this way, every moment of following the current, is a window you go through. As you miss the window, the current keeps unfolding the entirety in time, even though the whole object is there in space, without time.

The reason you want a window is that there's something your want in the *room*.

If it's success that you missed, you might still get another as the current unfolds. It's not the same one success. But does it matter? If it's a person that you missed, you might become with that person again. Yet people changes. Therefore it's not the same person with the same story anymore. But how does it matter? If you want something badly, feel deeper through that something. Underneath this appearing wave of wanting, what is it that you are deeply moved towards?

Let's do a brief exercise. Now, feel the entire appearance, your thoughts, your life story, all objects around you. Feel outside this room, outside this city, continent. What's the texture of the dirt on the moon right now? Feel as far as you can feel into the galaxy. That unchanging space is knowing these words. As you are going outward, also feel inward of you. Feel infinity and your inner field as much as you can, simultaneously. This is the dissolution of boundary. This is life's entirety here not in time but in space.

Now, answer this:

Why do you choose success? Why do you choose any Woman? The world *her* and the human *her*. Underneath the appearing waves of thoughts, emotions, situations, objects whose existences may not be as solid as you assume, beyond the sense of identity, the need for completion, do you still want any of *her*? The success, the world and the woman. What do you want fundamentally? Beyond the fluctuating appearances, what you are truly moved towards in *her* might not be what you have been clinging onto. Feel that current that is moving you, see whether it's moving you beyond the appearing flow of thoughts. If it isn't, don't move, stay with it with alertness. If it is so, get up.

Allow yourself to be moved, lived by this force without obstruction without holding back. It's leading you somewhere, it's leading you towards a *her* you truly want beyond all appearances. Even if it's not the exact same *her* that you thought you wanted in the first place. Does it matter at all?

Keep feeling the current that is unfolding the entirety for you. Meanwhile, cultivate the capacity to surf the appearing waves. Stop waiting, be ok to do nothing, but don't hesitate when the wind picks up. The *her* in the *room*, you may or may not get to.

Trust the current, learn to navigate its expression. You will be taken to the window if it's still a part of the entirety, to be unfolded in the future. If not, you will land on somewhere else just as profound.

On the other hand, if you don't keep moving with the current, but cling on to the window that you have missed, by hitting against that glass wall of time, you will never encounter another window down the unfolding entirety, only through which you might find what you have missed.

So do you try to do anything at all?
Yes. But we have to answer the next question first.

What do you mean by "stop waiting"?
Stop waiting means to stop hitting your head on the window-pane. You can hit on it forever yet still not getting through, though there are chances that you happen to hit in through a window by luck.

It's important to understand that taking action doesn't mean to take action in direct response to the appearing *flow*, your thoughts, situations, emotions, craves, agonies. You will have no idea what action is right that can get you to a better place.

To stop waiting means to feel the entirety of this *current* deeper than the *flow*. The current expresses itself as the appearing waves, but is multidirectionally beyond appearances.

Chances are that we are still waiting for something. We secretly believe that if something happens, our state of happiness will change fundamentally. We think we have to get somewhere, something, someone before we can be happy.

A fly hits on the glass over and over. It can't see the window, whereas the window is apparent to us. Yet we are doing the exact irony. Only for us, the windowpane is called time.

Chapter 13:
The Spirit of Sex

45.

"Hey I Know You"

_The Making of Spiritual Love

Bodies are doing their thing. Consciousness stands free. All forms are one to begin with, yet they appear to be separate. In sex, consciousness is fucking light's movement. Perceiving as consciousness, you contain light's continuing reformation showing through a woman. Exposed as love, she trusts the contemplation from you. When she flows like liquid, you are drawn to become the space for her evolution. When you see her inside out, she lets go of control revealing nature's will to blossom her body. Your practice is to access and sustain consciousness, looking straight into love, not distracted by your own enjoyment. Her practice is to be love, not disrupting nature's force with personal tension.

You are the river bank that can't be carried away by the river; she is the crystal-thin water that contains no mud. If you are distracted, you will join her flow, becoming part of the river. Then the river will have no space to continue. You both will become a pond sinking into the thickness of swamp. If she carries a baggage of rocks, if she prefers to form her own direction, the river will be blocked by her angularity and you will both turn into structures with no flow. You will become a dry bank with no interest in her rocks. For nature to dance, the masculine has to vacuum out depth, and the feminine has to fill this depth with flow. If sex is delightful but shallow, the masculine needs to create more space through the contemplation of death. If sex turns rigid and boring, the feminine needs to offer more energy through the expression of life.

Flow creates the bank and bank leads the flow. They have to exist together, and yet stay opposite for either one to be. The wilder the river, the deeper the way. The deeper the way, the louder the water.

As the bank, you will be tempted to join her giggle. Yet if you do, she gets crept out and has to stop. As the river, she has to let go of her own rock, whose rigidity will challenge his structure. If the river wants the bank to stand for her, then she has to stop throwing rocks at him. The river has to trust the bank, reserving no control but just flowing like a slut. The bank has to contain the river, making no motion but just being the space for her sluttiness to explode. The strength of river bank is measured by the power of flow that he can contain without becoming flow himself. The potency of the masculine is measured by the sluttiness of the woman he can contemplate without becoming woman himself. The simultaneous opposition and mergence between wild energy and empty space is sex, in everything of nature.

Now consider, what makes the strongest river bank possible?

Any physical structure has a limit, but the destructing force of water is limitless. No matter how solid a rock is, there is always a force carried by water that can crush it, flush it away and grind it to dust. All material containers' capacities have maximums, but flow's force can be infinite. How can you stay uncollapsable then?

The only thing that is impossible to be carried away, is no thing. Space never resists, but always contains. River's force cannot disturb space. And because of the absence of resistance, the river can increase its energy exponentially in the infinite orgasm. Space is the ultimate container. To contain a woman's pleasure without end, to not be carried away and stop the river completely through ejaculation, the only way that she can unendingly increase sexual desire is for you to not join in and therefore make the flow muddy. You become space, always knowing her, always caressing her, always containing her, and yet allowing her to evolve, never distracted by the beauty of her flesh.

Not able to destroy the bank's structure into pieces, her sexual power will evolve louder, only to fuck you up and then blame how weak you are. All the while you stay the space that she is all-arounded by, but unable to attack. You become the selfless transparent awareness, that she is felt by and yet can't perturb. Women's body has infinite ability to sustain pleasure. Men will ejaculate once pleasure builds to body's limit. Every male body has a maximum capacity in containing pleasure, just like every river bank has its limit in containing flow. But women's pleasure can magnify infinitely, if the man is able to contain her, just like a river can be infinitely fast if the bank is capable to stand with no resistance. Sex is a way for bodies to reach infinity. Infinity can't be reached by men's pleasure, you can get closer, but not a chance that the force of desire flowing through a male body can be as frighteningly miraculous as a woman's pleasure. We men are boats in the ocean, we like to think that we possess power. LOL. Women are the ocean. Boats cannot overpower the ocean. The only thing that is not afraid of tsunami is the space where the tsunami occurs. For space, any force expressed by the ocean is just like a teasing strip dance. *"Cute. Show me more. Interesting."*

Space is fucking everything. Over 99.9% of every biological human body is space, not to mention the subtle body of emotion and mind. Consciousness is penetrating existence constantly. You are fucked by it too. Unless, you become it. Then your body, her body, every body, is just doing biological strip dance for you, while you are inside of everything. This place is a freaking paradise, if you know how to *be*. Yet every place in every realm –dreaming, waking or after-dying– is the same paradise, because space is always there. Wherever there is a thing, there has to be a place for that thing to show up. As long as anything becomes, it is instantly fucked by space. Have you ever wonder why enlightened sages don't need women? Because those mother fuckers are screwing every existing qualitative Ding 24/7, for billions of years non-ending and even before that. If you have never be of consciousness, your life is a stressful constipation. You think that the more you tense up your ass, the more powerful your will be. Meanwhile, 99.9% of your tensed ass is still space. Therefore, you are now being fff... To spare your pride, we won't say it. How do you not be F-ed? The only way out, is to be the cosmic fucker yourself. And you don't even have to change a thing. You are already the ultimate fucker. It's just that every time you are distracted by existence, you turn into manifestation which is always fucked. Every time you are distracted by women's flesh, you virtually become a woman yourself, holding up your ass high.

Now, let's go back to the beginning of this article, even before the river bank story. There should have been an opening scenario with your sweetheart:

In the bedroom, you look into each other. You see yourself is her, and both know something that can't be put into words – the unsayable mutual acknowledgment of same identity. As if from another place, you both are on earth to fulfill a game. Bodies are machines, through which you come to know one another. You see her inside her appearing form and she does you the same. Without contact, you have already merged with her. Two bodies are so aware of one another's feeling that have become one. The rest is an expression. Two selves of the one knowing express this merged love through emotion and flesh. Humorous and artistic.

Bodies are doing their thing. Consciousness knows itself in the other.

46.

Zen and the Art of Sex

There are three levels of sex: Gross, Subtle, and Causal. On the Gross level, physical friction is performed by bodies made of meat and skin. To the next, romance and emotional connection happen in the subtle realm. In the end, sex of the soul is the mutual acknowledgment of the only self who the two persons both are.

If you are unable to connect with her on the Subtle level or Causal level, you're either going to ejaculate fast, or just doing mechanical pumps.

The goal of Gross-level sex is ejaculation. It's how bodies replicate. However, to conserve energy from leaking, you have to shift awareness into the subtle realm or the causal realm. If you can't have sex with someone emotionally or spiritually, don't have sex. Gross-level sex alone is a burst to depletion. The whole thing becomes shitty. Emotional fuck and spiritual fuck can last for hours or even days. In fact, genital inter-course is not even a necessity. Physical fuck is an add-on, to do *through*, not to get lost into. Fuck is happening in all realms. You can fuck with someone who has a fuckable intelligence, a fuckable emotional complex, a fuckable energetic expression, a fuckable heart, with or without thrusting in pussy. Physical pussy is additional.

For men and women, here are our gifts and tendencies when it comes to sex:

Women are usually more sensitive to the subtle realm. The emotional fuck is usually a prerequisite for genital sex. They need romance and connection. They read romance novels while we watch porn.

Men are Gross. Our awareness stays in the physical realm if undeveloped. We tend to lock attention onto pussies and racks. It really doesn't matter if romance is involved or not. A man can put his dick into a whole on a wall regardless of who's on the other side. We get horny on body parts and mechanical movements.

However, our real domain is the Causal realm. Masculine humans are embodiments of consciousness. We are inherently not at home in the physical or emotional realm. Only when we are disconnected with who we truly are beyond life, are we reducing interest to the Gross level of sex. Once a man bypasses the Gross identification, he gets into the Causal realm. A completely conscious man can fuck a woman to trembling just by looking at her across the room. That kind of fuck is impersonal. It is happening in every instant of perception. The men's practice is to embody it, so that his presence reminds a woman that she is light, as well as reminds other men of their mutual depth.

When such a man has genital sex with a woman. He is not wallowed by sensations. It becomes a fuck of spirit.

So how does a man shift his awareness from Gross to Causal?
By widening attention. Physicality is a condensed manifestation. The place that contains it, is causality. As you expand attention to feel more and further, all at once, you eventually become aware of space. Space is what causes this whole shit show. It is the ultimate causality.

An effective practice to free attention from mental image and genital arousal is to feel the aliveness of desire with your whole body. Instead of focusing on what's in your head and dick, feel your entire body. Energetically speaking, you should feel arousal from your perineum to the base of spine, instead of the base of penis. This allows energy to go up in circulation. If you find yourself fantasizing sexual images, you can intentionally breathe down energy from your head.

As you become aware of your internal energy flow and breathing, your attention comes to the subtle domain. Now you can expand this sensitivity to your woman's body. Notice her tension or undulation. How the energy flows in her body? How deep is her breath? Does she tense up eyes and neck? Are her wrists relaxed and arms open? Most people are completely unaware of their own tension. This is where you paint your masterpiece. You can actually feel combining your energetic body with hers, using fingers and tongue to guide her energy from base of spine up to the neck. Imagine your eyes conduct silk-like touch wherever you look to soften her eyes. Breathe to her rhythm so that you occupy the same emotional space, and then gently take the lead increasing breath's depth.

She will feel well-fucked but likely have no idea what you have done. This should be every man's art. Nothing on earth comes more responsive than a fluid woman.

This subtle emotional domain is where magical moments happen. It can be done throughout the day or during sex. It's women's domain, and we are invading it to align her emotions.

This could be good enough. But it's not the end. We men don't just stay in the subtle realm. Once our attention shifts from Gross to Subtle, it burst into Causal space of presence like a bubble.

That is where we feel who we are at ease. What traps us is the distraction of pleasure. If the traps are overcome, we get out. Men can't feel the sense of mission in the energy domain. Our ultimate home is all the way to emptiness, free from physicality and energy all together. The feeling out of freedom is that *"I am already dead. Nothing will make me happy or sad. Let me make art to her through the offering of fuck, because she is the only light."*

At this time, you are not only energetically combining with her, but also holding space for her. Space is fucking its won manifested light. Big bang. Now you two are fucking physically, energetically, and with spirit. It's the fullest sense of sex, as good as it gets.

Then here's a nuance that can make or break the experience of going all the way. This time it's on the woman's part.

To have sex with spirit in the Causal level. You need to be consciousness itself and she needs to be light energy.

That light energy can expand to fill space, or be reduced into a body. For women, there is a big difference between *"my body-and-emotion is being fucked"* and *"I am being fucked"*. When all she feels is her body-and-emotion being fucked by another body-and-emotion, sex stops on the subtle level. It is better than just physical sex without energy merging, but not as complete as the fuck of conscious-light.

Women identify with energy just like men identify with body parts. It's addictive. Men and women at difference developmental stages find themselves at the following levels:

- The lowest level is the pumping motion of two genitals.
- The middle level is the merging of energetic essence.
- The highest level is the realization of who we are and what has always been. Time can't be perceived in such a state.

Men are trapped in level one. Women are trapped in level two.

Although men can jump to level three from wherever they are, they can also skillfully bypass through level two. Once you are in level two, you naturally slide into level three. Once you are in level three, the art in level two becomes self-manifesting.

For women, it's equally tempting to stay at the default level.

Sex in the domain of inner being is comfortable. Why bother to go to spirit? For women to connect with men's causal consciousness, she has to realize something. That realization makes her usual comfort from sexual merging seem insignificant.

It takes courage and trust — and sometimes unbearable suffering of not enough — for her to leave the private snuggles behind and be open as love.

She has to feel herself as what's even more than an emotional entity. She needs to realize that the self that is being penetrated is the boundless light that is beyond her body and emotion. A fundamental *quality* is being fucked by a *capacity* to know this *quality*. She has to feel who she is beyond the fairytale of princess. She is the light with no shape.

The energetic exchange of body continues, but she is opening outward instead of curling inward to a personal pleasure. She looks at you. You look at her. You both know. Neither she or you know what it is that you know. Words fall short. As sex continues, you look at each other, you both know.

47.

5-Hour Porn Star

_Meditation and Ejaculation Control

The key to non-ejaculation sex is to feel the bigger-than-life empty space. It means to expand your attention. Awareness can't be fixed on your own pleasure, insecurity, or even the objective of non-ejaculation.

Consciousness is what stays absolutely still behind all motion. When you feel pleasure, consciousness doesn't move; when you feel pain, consciousness stays still. But as pleasure or pain comes, we get wrapped in our own sensations. Distracted by sensory stimulation, we get up attending to happenings. Our attention becomes narrowed onto thoughts, body parts, or maybe a paper cut on the finger.

Ejaculation is to leak out energy in a spasmatic release. Your nature as consciousness is always at ease, though you might assume yourself to be a separated solidity that exists among other solidities, seeking for release into freedom. Consciousness is free, even though your body-and-mind often accumulates tension. This tension makes you want to let out energy through ejaculation, talking, and excessive thinking. Tension can only exist in the realm of manifestation, under the watch of empty space.

Once you can feel as the conscious spaciousness, you are free and no longer seeking for release. To bypass the urge to ejaculate is to access consciousness, which is who we really are but we tend to forget, which has no tension to be released.

It's good to feel whatever you are experiencing entirely. But you should also be feeling the part of you that is able to feel. Instead of feeling the pleasure, feel feeling itself.

During sex, you can expand attention by feeling pleasure with your whole body, instead of just penis. Be aware of the body in mutual contact of hands, arms, belly, back, legs and feet. Expand this much first, and then keep expanding outward as far as you can. All the while try to listen to the sound as far as you can, outside the bedroom, on the freeway, in the forests. Try to hear another continent and the breeze on the surface of moon. Being aware of everything internal and external at once.

You can also expand your attention by feeling into your woman's pleasure so thoroughly that you forget your own. If you can really feel her pleasure, you will find out that her pleasure is always bigger than yours.

Consciousness doesn't have a boundary. When you are as the part of you that can feel and know, that can't be distracted by happenings, who you are expands. You are no longer an isolated person in a body separated from the rest of the world by your skin. Imagine you are a race car driver or rock climber. As you are making a high-speed turn on the edge of a cliff, or making a big leap grabbing the corner of a rock with one hand, you become transcended into perception itself. That is the feeling of being consciousness. No matter whatever extreme is happening, your capacity to know stays still.

Your practice in sex is to access this part of you. Yet beyond meditative consciousness, the other side of training is about internal energy.

The reason you come short is that your energy stagnates in the genital area to a point where it has to leak out. Internal energy is often stuck in the head or dick. When you are caught up on your own philosophical experiment in the head, you lose erection. When you are caught up on your own pleasure that your dick is in a warm wet hole, your energy is stagnated. If you keep stimulate without circulating, all men will ejaculate at one point.

Bodily speaking, the key to ejaculation control is to circulate energy. Pull the energy in your dick up through spine to your head, and then down to your chest and lower belly into your genitals again. Your sexual energy will increase as stimulation goes on. But there won't be a point that you have to ejaculate as long as you can handle this energy by actively circulating it.

This active circulation is directed with consciousness and body both. Energy stagnates in your penis because you are attending to your own pleasure. When your dick is being sucked wet, you are not going to care whether the coffee cup is leaving a stain on the table. All your attention is narrowed onto the sensation on your dick. As your entire body tense up, circulation stops. All energy goes to your dick until it can't handle it anymore and ends your erection with a shot. Then you feel released, free of constraints. Sex is over.

The first key to prolong sex is to expand your attention. The reason that you have to come is that the energy in your genitals has been accumulated to the limit. And the reason it is accumulated is that you put too much attention on the sensation of pleasure. The root of energy stagnation is narrowed attention.

There are countless ways to expand your attention. Most time of the day, our attention is on our own well-being. Our feeling, our money, our identity, our sensation. When dick is sucked, you habitually focus on the pleasure. To be consciousness is to free your attention so that you feel your body, her body, the room, the coffee on the table, books on the shelf, and still aware of your pleasure.

To free your attention, you can feel into her body. Noticing the placement of her ankle, are her eyes tense or softened, is her neck vulnerable or protected, are her arms open to expose her front or closed covering her stomach. To guide another human being into surrender, you will need to be aware of her subtle feeling of surrender or resistance, which changes in every second. By feeling her waves of pleasure, you free attention from your own sensation.

You are here having sex, maybe in a beach house listening to the waves pounding seashore. But right now, you could have been on the gnarling ocean in a small boat with a broken engine. Alone in the dark as wave picks up. Wind blows loud, rain is pouring on your skull. Your boat is a tiny dot on the ocean. Your mast is down on the deck as you pulling the rope on a small sail trying to move without engine. You tie up another life jacket, looking at city lights on the coast twenty miles away. Your adrenaline pumps up as you ride over another high wave. Storm's coming, no one knows you are here…

Enjoy your sensations, but at the same time, feel what it would be like to be alone on the sea in the dark beholding a coming storm.

You can now feel as far as you can to another continent.

In this moment, there are people starving and watching their family being murdered. As you are enjoy a tender wet hole, some are being kidnapped and abused. Some people are in torturous pain dying in the hospital. Their loved ones are watching them dying in agony yet can't do anything to even share the agony. Right now as you are feeling pleasure on your dick, all these are also happening…

You can feel time in fast-forward. As your dick is sucked. Look are the motion of pushing and pulling of her lips, her eyes sparkling, hair spreading on her shoulder and breasts upright. But we are dying. In the life span of this universe, 4 minutes and 40 years makes no difference. We will die in forty years, or maybe four minutes. This woman is sucking your dick because she loves you. But you are both dying. Fast-forward your life-time together, or fast-forward your life-time apart and then reconnect in decades.

She's sucking your dick as wrinkles begin to form on her forehead. Her sparkling eyes become tired and angular. Her hair that used to spread softly around her neck is turning gray and dry. Her lips are no longer youthful and delicious. Her breasts shrink into loose skin hanging on a hunched body. Forty years in four minutes. You are both old. You look into her eyes. Her devotion to love is still the one of the little girl forty years ago. Through her suffer, the love in her still wants to find a way to come through.

And now come back when you both have youth. You are hard and strong. Her lips are soft and juicy. You look into her eyes...

Her hair spreads on the pillow, arms open. She's screaming in pleasure letting go of who she is. This person might have been abandoned before, been cheated before. Her parents might have left her in an early age. Her father might have been abusive. She might have given up on love. She had suffered the futility of life, just like you have. Yet in this moment, love comes through her. Her devotion has led her beyond fear to be in this moment with you. Her vulnerably surrender to your penetration is the trust of love. And you are the man that is going to answer all her fear and doubts that yes love exists. There's nothing but only love that prevails. In this moment you are the one that heals her wound, open her heart to face unknown future of happiness and pain. You are the one that gives her enlightenment, right here, in her.

There are endless ways to expand attention beyond your own body. Even lesser techniques such as thinking about sandwich or visualize running a marathon would work temporarily. When you attention is free from your own sensation, you are consciousness, you are free.

48.

Are We There Yet?

_The Part of Sex Before Orgasm

At some point, you will likely to realize that chasing after pleasure is deeply unsatisfying. Hormones are rushing through your body to keep you in the cycle of building up tension and spasmatic leaking. Ejaculation is something proper if you want to make babies. Other than that, it drains your life force and dulls your spirit. That feeling of unenthusiasm and depletion after an ejaculation, we all know. Genetically, woman are evolved to nurture babies. Their bodies are developed to circulate internal energy in order to have a lush home for the baby. We men are evolved to shoot out life essence. There are wild salmons in Alaska that die immediately after an ejaculation. We have more shots than salmons, but it leads to the same end eventually. Have you tried to orgasm 10000 time in a day? Why don't you give it a go and come back to tell me on Halloween.

That thing called semen is able to create offspring for a reason. It is the essence of your body. It's the most valuable asset energetically. To remain creativity and clarity, to have vision and humor, we need to learn to circulate that energy, which women are already good at for biological reasons.

Orgasm is a very stubborn addiction. It is learned through decades of neurological habits that wasn't considered harmful. When you realize the addiction and its negative effects, it has become too ingrained in the body to break. Now you have a well-trained addictive pattern, plus daily produced hormone. Good luck to you.

Once a man retrains his nervous system, sex becomes a whole-body experience. It is not felt as explosively good as a peak orgasm. But when you are having sex in the subtle and causal realm, you want to stay in it. You don't want to go back to the spasm that ends it all. You want to keep in the subtle and causal sex for days long after the genital friction. Physical ejaculation becomes an insignificant pleasure of which you suddenly lose interest.

At this point, sex becomes an offering. While women become enlightened by flowing with life's force, men often approach enlightenment from understanding. Sex is to have her experience you for her enlightenment. And you have to be expressing love through every cell of the body. I wouldn't recommend you to have your sexual partner sit down with you while you lecture her on the philosophical conflict depicted in Bhagavad Gita. But you can show what you have learned in the Gita by pinning her down with overwhelming love and fucking her to truth.

Compassion and understanding are important for men to have, for the sake of retraining ourselves off ejaculation addiction. Our attention is so easily focused on physical and visual pleasure. You can have a wide open awareness and in the very next second reduce all your consciousness to a contraction of vagina. Compassion is from heart, while ejaculation is from cock. Understanding is about bringing energy to the heart, the center, so that mental contraction of fantasizing and prostatic contraction of ejaculation can be overcome. It's always important to use your heart in everything throughout life, but especially sex. How you fuck women is a condensed representation of how you treat the world. Creep in the cock and greed in the head is most men's life and sex life.

If you have accustomed to shitty sex. To bring it to the subtle level at least means to have genuine compassion towards her in your heart. It doesn't matter whether you have been partner with this person for ten years or you just met her, you have to know her in truth. It's ok if you know nothing *about* her. The moral standards are the first thing you need to trash for the sake of enlightenment. Knowing has nothing to do with knowing about. You can know nothing about that person while knowing her completely. That complete knowing is what makes gross-level orgasm not urgent anymore. This knowing is a capacity you can develop by acknowledging the being-ness in everything you come in contact with. It is a practice on your part.

The good news is, although sex is the biggest distraction, it's also the best practice to feel another being. Your practice is to see through form even in the most outrageous sexual acts. From flirting to intercourse, feel deeper than her flesh and then communicate with her inner-most being. While conversation isn't absolutely necessary prior to sex, it can be a good source for you to feel her from.

If you can comprehend what her life is, how she was brought up, how she was treated as kid in school, what her fear and dreams are, what gave her the courage to go so far... it will evoke your strength to protect. This is an instinct for masculine beings to take care of our bitches. When you have this sponta-neous compassion, you will be able to really taste and breathe her life as if it has a flavor. When you can taste this flavor of her, you will know what you can give to her. What is the quality that she doesn't have in her life, where is it that she has never been taken? You will instantly know what experience to bring her that can make her life instantly better. You know this with perceptive intuition, not mental analysis.

During sex, she is letting go of her structure and trusting yours. Where it goes, gentle or brutal is led by you. And you have to see the whole process as if it is in space, so that you can instantly know what is needed in this moment without trial and error in time. *Knowing about* her life is not crucial for good sex, but it is very helpful for you to *know* her. A woman has a unique energetic quality, and you will be able to feel what she would taste like if she was a pie. That is a very important knowing that keeps you in the subtle communion or even causal acknowledgment.

49.

No-fap for You

_Training for Self Discipline

C elibacy should be a by-product. If you are single, this is a perfect period in your life to practice celibacy. You probably haven't stopped ejaculating on a frequency since adolescence. Later on in life, you realize that to be a good person requires discipline. It might just be flashes of thoughts, eventually forgotten. Most people lived their lives without expressing their gifts. Our potentials vary, and all have value to the entirety. Some are here to design spaceships, some are here to sit on a chair laughing and make people happy, some are here to meditate in caves to hold humanity's awareness. All of those greatness requires discipline.

What is the best training available for self mastery then?

It is the relationship with your hormonal impulse.

For people who are in sexual relationships, it's quite difficult to retrain both partners' patterns at once. But if you are single, you have no excuse not to cultivate the greatest virtue of all time – self discipline. This is going to be a horrendous journey. You will go through trial and error, success and failure. It might take years. But in the end, what you will learn is not to suppress desires, but to access your deeper truth, and to sustain that vision. You will learn what kind of situation and life habits you should be in. You align life gradually to have a beneficent environment for mental and bodily clarity.

Celibacy is not the goal necessarily. But a target to aim for. You will have to master the game of desire, life and spirit to reach it. When you get to the end, you will be awake and clear. You will be able to manage your daily matters as well as long-term career. And then, you can expand this ability to others, to align their life with your clarity and discipline. When you have a group of people working together, or when you get to raise a family, they will be able to follow your guidance with complete trust.

50.

The Origin of Sexual Art

As you are learning spirituality and sexuality. The word Tantra might come along at some point. Surrounded by misunderstanding, I want to get into the origin of Tantra briefly.

Tantra is short for Tantrayana, which is another word for Vajrayana. In India, people often use the term Tantra while in Tibet it becomes Vajra. They are rooted in very similar disciplines if not identical. Tantra is distinct from Sutra in Hindu Yoga, while Vajrayana is distinct from Hinayana and Mahayana in Buddhism. Sutra, Hinayana and Mahayana are the foundations. Tantra and Vajrayana are likely to be messed up by us people. But this comes later.

In the west, Tantra is being regarded as a series of sexual skills. Like a secret lost martial art. It is not. Tantra is not here to give us more pleasure, but to build up discipline in the midst of pleasure. Many people get into Tantra because they are looking for a whole-body orgasm as Tantra promised.

Yes you do get whole-body orgasms through Tantric training, even throughout the day. By that orgasm has nothing like a genital orgasm where your pudendal nerve is triggered. Nothing in the domain of physics will feel as stimulating as a genital orgasm which you have already experienced thousands of times. If peak pleasure is all that you are after, Pornhub is a good place to start.

Tantra is to feel *through* physical stimulation, transcending it into the acknowledgment of God, or conscious-light.

It feels right when you are seeing conscious-light. You won't want it any other way. But before you have felt it, you might still be swiping Tinder. The discipline is in riding the wave of stimulation. Similar to surfing, where the bigger the wave, the faster you fly. You want stimulation but not to drown in the stimulation. Most people that seek feeling-good in Tantra is looking to be drowned.

Many spiritual readers still consider eastern practice as about peace and compassion. It is, yet it doesn't stop there.

Major bookstores often stock texts on Hinduism, Buddhism, Zen and Taoism. This collection is the equivalent of western study of cognitive science. In science we speculate, while in spirit we see. Hinduism is one of the origins of eastern spiritual traditions. It evolved into Buddhism, which was brought to China, then Vietnam and Thailand. It spreads into three major schools: Hinayana, Mahayana and Vajrayana. Hinayana is about accessing peace by withdrawing attention from the world. No matter how fucked up the situation is, you can always reside as pristine consciousness that is fundamentally peaceful. It is widely practiced in Thailand. Being present as consciousness is emphasized by many great contemporary teachers, though they are also well-trained in the other two traditions. Mahayana is the Buddhism in China. It is where the practice of compassion comes from. A Mahayana practitioner sees the world as an expansion of the self. Instead of drawing back attention abandoning the externals, they practice breathing in others' suffer and offering blessing to everyone.

Question: Do monks have sex?
In Hinayana and Mahayana, you shouldn't. It's distraction. You want peace and compassion, and sex is nasty. In Vajrayana, *yes baby!* Big waves make happy surfers. Sex becomes an approach to access peace and compassion. Instead of withdrawing from lust and anger, you can stand right in it, magnifying lust and anger to a point where the narrowing tension is released open. Right though the doorway of evil distraction, you find peace. It could be a fucked-up, dysfunctional, self-destructive peace. In such a practice, you may appear to live like a slut, a weirdo, an alcoholic, a pervert, and yet completely enlightened, transmitting love through perversions. However this makes Vajrayana

the least practiced tradition in the east. Vajrayana and its equivalent Tantrayana are mostly taught in Tibet and India.

Nowadays we start to learn from it in the west. The heavy amount of involvement in a dirty world makes Hinayana and Mahayana excluded, yet Tantra sounds cool enough.

Sex and drugs can be an expression of Vajrayana discipline. But they shall be done as a sacrifice of hard-achieved wholeness, instead of a greedy pleasure to indulge. If you still have even the slightest question whether to stay sober or drink, whether to do drugs or not, whether to have sex or stay celibate, then you shouldn't drink, do drug or fuck. If the neediness in any of those activities presents, it will take you over in abuse. And the motive to indulge becomes very ambiguous: *am I fucking to create love in the world, or to stimulate that nerve in the penis?* And you will likely to ejaculate in the end, which is often a selfish exploit that doesn't have any compassion rippling outwards. You will always think *"well, I'll just come this time and start to discipline tomorrow."* Next thing you know is that you are a sex addict under the noble sign of Tantra. The same sign covers up alcoholics and drug addicts.

Tantra is to stay in the world's complication and give love as a complication. It takes tremendous discipline that is sourced in Hinayana and Mahayana practices. If we can't be absolutely present facing a wall, we won't be able to do it inside a woman's body, or under the influence of alcohol. Sex and alcohol are distracting. If we can't have compassion to a stranger on the street, we won't be concerning about a woman's feeling as we are about to burst that little puddle of sperms. Presence and compassion have to be there for any Tantra to start at all. Not everyone is ready for Tantra and Vajra. And that's really fine. If you still have doubt whether to fuck or not will be good for your practice, chances are that you are not quite ready. Then you have two choices: one is to have sex that's likely ending in ejaculative contraction anyway, and the other is to go back to your meditation cushion cultivating wholeness in solitude. When you are conscious and compassionate, there will be no ambiguity on the to-fuck-or-not-to-fuck question.

It is completely fine if you just want to have some normal sex where you can come in the end. People are doing it every day, right now, your parents did it, and the world is still a beautiful place. There are hobbyists and artists. Everyone can sing in the shower and car, and they don't have to be professionals. But if you choose to create the masterpiece of singing, you will have to do that ugly lip-roll warm-up every morning, and discipline your diet, sleep, exercise to maintain a healthy vocal chord.

Right now I'm thinking some of the people I know. Their lives are hard enough for them to have a BBQ and chill on a Saturday afternoon. I really don't want to induce them to practice the sacrifice of Tantrayana. Going back home and rubbing genitals are relaxing and good enough for most people.

However, if you have the karma to be motivated in the art of giving love through sexual offer. Here are some suggestions to start the treacherous training with.

51.

The Way of Pleasure

Perhaps no one has told you this, but in the training of Vajrayana or Tantrayana, discomfort should be applied as much as pleasure. Pleasure often gets practitioners lost in gratification without realizing it. Pain and pleasure can both be used as a test from the temporary display of appearances. However it's difficult to tell if the indulgence in pleasure is for practice or driven by craving. If pleasure itself is still pleasurable to you at all, you shouldn't euphonize the weakness in self control under a glorious name of spirituality. External stimulation should only be considered when renunciation of sensory satisfaction has been practiced throughly. Only then should the test of appearing display be utilized, as in both pleasure and pain.

Unless you are indifferent in pleasure and pain, your so-called Vajrayana practice is just mind's rationalization for seeking sensory gratification, while adding an ego identification in practicing the highest school of eastern tradition. It is so common to see people kidding themselves, hiding behind to shield of a grand and yet supposedly treacherous endeavor, while secretly cling to the ordinary pleasure of senses.

How do you know whether you are ready to step into the world of pleasure from meditation cushion?

Try the next exercise first.

52.

Be Free from Sensations

_Awareness in Cold Shower

S tepping into a cold shower can be a discipline of spirit. Our mind is constantly wandering off. Once the cold water hits you, attention is forced back to bodily awareness rather than mind's activity. Without putting attention on mind's movement, the movement stops. You silence the mind by putting yourself into extreme sensations.

This method to bring yourself back to body awareness is used in Tantric practice. However Tantra implies pleasurable sensations. It is about using pleasure to draw your attention from head down to the lower chakras. Yet there is one thing wrong that we can commit to — indulgence. When pleasure comes, we tend to lose ourselves in it. We give in and give up, allowing pleasure to take us to mediocrity. In Tantra, ejaculation is the ultimate failure of practice. Tantra is gaining its popularity in the modern world, due to the emphasize on magnifying pleasure. However, we forget to mention that only when you are free from sensations, can you allow pleasure to happen yet not be distracted.

Let's look at pleasure and pain, using the example of sex. Someone touches your nipple, you feel pleasure. She squeezes harder, you are more turned on. If she keeps squeezing with increasing force, to a point this pleasure is going to turn into pain. Happenings and sensations are natural, they are just direct experiences on a scale from pain to pleasure. To be able to stay present without distraction, you have to train to be free in pain. In this practice, it is the discomfort of cold water.

If you are drawn to experience pleasure at all, you are clearly not free from it. Only when you can stop grasping, fantasizing, exaggerating, remembering pleasurable experiences, are you ready to encounter them as they rise. Tantric practice should not start in the bedroom, but rather in the adversity of sensations. Instead of indulging yourself in comfort, you can be forced into freedom because cold water will cause suffering if you are not free from it. In sex, if you are caught up on physical pleasure, you ejaculate. Whereas in cold shower, if you are caught up on physical discomfort, you suffer. Sex is the test, ordeal is the training ground.

To put yourself in a cold shower, you need determination first. There has to be a decision of walking in that cold water. Your emotion is trying to stay away. Therefore to do it at all, dis-identification with emotion is the first step. It happens not in a distant way that you no longer feel emotions. Rather, you feel the cold air around the shower beam as well as your unwillingness to step in, but you do it anyway. The dis-identification with emotions signals your residence in consciousness.

Dealing with energy while being consciousness, now we are training. The feeling of staying in discomfort is that you are looking straight ahead. Not to the left of discomfort, nor to the right for warmth. The concept of cold and warm becomes flat, you are staying right there, feeling whatever is completely, while knowing straight ahead beyond sensations. This is also the proper disposition in dealing with sexual stimulus.

As in this practice, cold water first brings you back to your body awareness, stopping your thinking, drawing your attention from thoughts to feelings. This is also what sex can do. It's important to point out that good sex is not the same as fantasizing pornographic imagery. When you are fantasizing, you are stuck in your head. Good sex is a whole-body experience, when you are intimate with another person, your body's intelligence is awake. Bodies will find it's rhythm to move, without mind's thinking at all. Therefore sex is a great practice for bodily awareness.

However, sex is pleasurable and tempting, your attention can be wrapped around physical stimulation, and therefore consciousness gives in. You get lost in the good feelings physically and emotionally. As a man, once you get lost in sexual sensations, your attention gets locked on body parts and isolated pleasure in your genital area. Then you ejaculate and deplete energy. This leakage is unnecessary unless your goal is to make babies.

To be able to stay conscious in intense sensations, you'd better off train with discomfort than pleasure. No one is tempted to get lost in the feeling of icy cold. You want to get out of it. To stay in it without suffering, you have no other way but to be present with what is, to be highly conscious. You feel the cold ever more completely, but not just the discomfortable effect of it. You feel the texture of the cold water and breathe this texture in your lungs. Here, you are practicing the art, which can later be transferred to love making as you feel the textural quality of the other person and breathe this quality in. You are training in a way that forces you to be in the right disposition, and there's no risk of failure as ejaculation in sex.

Chapter 14:
Meditative
Practice

53.

Three Types of
Meditation

B ecause this chapter is a series of meditative practice.
It's necessary to point out different types of meditation
that we do.

Traditional meditation training is always to find an access to
consciousness. It is about *nothing*. A practitioner often find himself sitting down facing a texturized wall, with no thoughts for
hours. It is a very effortless yet stressful experience. Effortless
because it is our default state of being. The mind crap can only
come afterwards. Stressful because we are too used to occu-
pying attention with motions. When motion stops, attention
becomes stagnated. In fact this discomfort from the stagnation

of attention is good. It soon leads to the expansion of attention, which is awareness.

In the west, meditation is often considered as something blissful. Well, if the nothing-ness of mind described above is blissful, then it is. But we tend to think that it leads to feeling-good, happiness. It doesn't. It is yet a fundamental default of joyful peace. Imagine you are alone on the sea for weeks starring at the horizon. It is peaceful and torturous and the same time. Many times meditation is a feeling of being tortured in a pleasurable way. Maybe for a few minutes in a thirty-minute session, you actually feel not having a body, not knowing anything yet completely aware of everything. We tend to psychologically or even physically grab onto something in those moments. But if we grasp, the purity of consciousness ends. So stay with it. It is being fucked by God, by the empty consciousness.

There is another kind called internal Yoga. There are many energetic exercises done internally without physical move-ments. In the modern days, these practices are considered meditation as well. The difference between traditional med-itation and internal Yoga is that Yoga is an *energy* training while meditation is a *consciousness* training. You must have a conscious awareness as the ground for Yoga, but energy doesn't need to flow in meditation. In Taoism tradition, meditation is considered as the energetic movement inside the body. This is a very different training than that of Tibetan Buddhism or Zen tradition. In Tibetan tradition, people do practice internal Yoga, but the recognition of consciousness is a completely different domain. If you have a physical injury, you can't perform some yoga exercises, internally or externally. However, you can be in any shape or form, or even in a dream as someone else, still recognizing consciousness.

Internal exercises are often practiced in Qigong, Chanting and Chakra Meditation. They can all be traced back to the Yoga tradition from India.

Besides Meditation of Consciousness and Internal Yoga, there is another form of meditation done as therapy. This type of session is often guided by a therapist or taped in a dreamy voice, "…Imagine you were a kid, walking into the house that you grew up. You enter one of the rooms, whom did you see…" Or "…Imagine you are in a happy place, you see yourself in twenty years standing in front of you. What would you say to him, what would he say to you…" This type of hypnotic session are also regarded as meditation by some people. These are therapies, to dig out your childhood issue or to reprogram a neurological response. They can be effective in psychological healing for your unresolved issues. But there is no recognition of consciousness or internal flow of energy being trained in here.

To wrap up, Meditation has been used to describe three types of practice – Conscious Meditation, Internal Yoga, and Therapy. The type of meditation introduced in this chapter is Conscious Meditation. It is the recognition of this moment's fundamental truth. You can do it regardless of your therapeutic health or energetic flow.

54.

Yoga and Consciousness

Any time you are directing internal energy with physical movement or mind, you are doing yoga, either you are moving or still. Any time you are trying to be present as the witnessing consciousness watching this moment appears and goes, you are doing meditation.

For most people the line between meditation and yoga is blurred. When a Taoist sits down to "meditate", he is actually doing internal Qigong, which is derived from yoga. When you lay back on the beach watching sea birds, witnessing the sound of ocean as if you are the space that contains this ocean, you are meditating. When a musician plays Blues guitar, transmitting conscious-light through his body onto the instrument, he is doing both meditation and yoga, with guitar skills added.

Yoga is to train your body to circulate abundant energy smoothly so that consciousness can express itself through human form. But you have to be consciousness first. If your body is weak or your energy channel is blocked, no matter how conscious you are, you can't use this consciousness to interact with people or surrounding environments. As an effect, your mind starts to stream negativity after this inadequate interaction. If your yoga is right on, which means you are circulating abundant energy, your mind is at ease. Therefore, it's less obstructive for you to access consciousness.

Consciousness itself is empty and therefore doesn't have a quality to be felt. But its residence in human body can be felt in regions of body and as variations of quality. You can practice feeling consciousness in your belly, spine, heart, solar plexus, up above your head, and even legs and crotch. These localized residence of awareness influence your posture and voice. A tribal warrior, a James Bond, a rock star, a king, a God, they represents the same consciousness through different qualities. Those expressions of awareness is the practice of art.

Yoga can draw your attention from gross realm to the subtle realm, which is one step closer to conscious causality. This is the contribution of yoga and Tai Chi to enlightenment. From gross to subtle to causal, what you are identified with becomes less and less condensed.

So, can yoga make you present?

Very likely so, but not necessarily. By utilizing the body, you begin to feel yourself in a body as presence. This presence is both consciousness and light.

55.

What Is Internal Energy?

O ur external reality consists of three components: materials, energy, and information. Everything you can touch is material, either it's a table in the living room, sand on the beach, water in the pool or your girlfriend's skin on your finger tip. Energy is stored in all objects. That's why wood can be burnt into fire. Light and sound are just waves vibrating to certain frequency which is information.

In modern science, material is considered as an appearing result of vibration. And since vibration is a result of energy and information, our external world can be considered as only energy and information.

Internal energy is also called Prana or Chi in various forms of Yoga. Scientists and fitness trainers study it as in the nervous system.

The intention to guide internal energy creates information. Information can be described and applied, but can't be detected through scientific instruments directly. Just like the number 45 can't be detected, even though you can detect 45 apples or elephants. The number 45 existing as pure information is undetectable, though applicable and describable. Modern scientific detection only applies to materials, frequencies and the dictation of information. Internal energy stands between information and physical energy. The majority of it remains under the radar from scientific approaches.

Then how does information affect your body and mind? Information can influence or even dictate your bodily reaction. Now, think about the juiciest boobs in the millennium, if you are good, you may get an erection. The deep visualization of boobs can affect your bodily response. In this case, the "juiciest boobs" exists only as information, applied through visualization to form a mental image, therefore dictating your blood flow to rush into your dick causing erection.

The key is to channel internal energy is to cultivate the capacity of visualization. Instead of visualize boobs, you visualize Chi.

If it's visualized, does it really exist?

If anything gives you an erection, you bet it exists. It may not exist as a solid object, but as information. The intention to lead Chi is a form of information that can affect you body. The subtle activities within and among the cells in your flesh can be dictated by this visualization, such as that of your dick.

56.

Think with Your Body, Act Immediately

_The First Principle of Yoga and Tai Chi

By thinking that internal energy has to be led by the mind, we unnecessarily assume that they are separate. Then we try to practice the effectiveness of them working together. But all you need to do is really just to relax and allow your subtle body-and-mind complex to move unobstructedly as it evolves. Allow nature to manifest itself. Body and mind function as a singular entity. When you allow them to be one, they sprint in accordance.

You are easily stuck in your head if trying to use mind to do ANYTHING.

Whenever possible, you should always act and think with your body, which is already blended with mind in creating the mixture of intelligence. This is how we act from intuition. If intuition has to be understood in the mind and then translated to the body, it's already altered and filtered.

Intuition has to be captured and acted upon instantaneously as it appears.

The only way to do this is to shorten the distance between mind and body, to a point that there's no distance.

When your mind is there, your body is there. The process of directing Chi should be a constant-refreshing instant reflex. The capacity to lead Chi is not necessarily a skill to develop, but the only right way to start training. When you're doing it, you don't even have the concept of Chi. Concepts are not necessary, yet the un-learning of such often is. When mind and body have no distance in between. They can function with no hesitation.

To act intuitively, you have to lose your mind completely. Mind is always an obstruction. Even the moment you attempt – with mind – to utilize mind to perform a specific task without mindstreaming, you are already distracted by the mind. The only way to live authentically is to act immediately, body and mind together, no hesitation. No thinking involved at all.

To remove mind obstruction, to be absolutely mad, you have to be the consciousness that is free falling, as if you suddenly become aware in a dreamless sleep.

Free will is an illusory sweet candy that doesn't count as food. You are not really controlling or channeling your life, or even controlling this moment. This moment is spontaneously *rising* as a spot on an interwoven web. You can simply choose to allow or resist. Sometimes it might seem that your forceful effort does make a difference, but the even the motivation for you to add effort is a part of this web that you can't see.

Killing the mindstream requires ruthlessness. Your mind, your memory, your rules shall be all killed. You then are simply ALLOWING. You then are allowing without the interference from mind. Body and mind will act by itself, by the will of God. Its force is unlimited. It will maneuver itself without you "thinking" of Chi.

You allow the ripple of the web, by killing your mind, by stopping thinking, by giving up controlling, by going crazy. You are a mad God already. Don't stop it because of fear. Go mad all the way.

57.

Meditation Exercise

When it comes to meditation, anything to be said is wrong. Meditation is to stop talking and thinking. When anything is being said, mind is engaged. Yet mind is the biggest obstruction of meditation. The best that words can do is to remind you of the feeling of meditation, the dissolution of self. Sometimes scriptures can be an effective reminder. But you have to do it for yourself to know. Sit down, see what happens. If nothing at all happens, you are doing it right.

There's nothing to be said about meditation. It is something to be realized and done spontaneously. But if we have to teach meditation skills, the best it gets is a guided practice of the embodiment of consciousness. Through the exercises, you can feel how consciousness coming through your human body. These feelings are to be experimented, explored and remembered by the nervous system. After months or even only weeks of practice, you should be able to access the conscious alertness most time during the day. It is not a permanent state, but a constant discipline. It takes lots of effort to practice, but the result of practice feels effortless.

Consciousness doesn't have any content for description, but the embodiment of it has. The training is a life-long discovery process for each individual. The following exercise is a good start.

This chapter is a guided meditation session. It can be a routine to start the day with. When you go through the exercise for the first time, read one section at a time and try to feel it as a first-person experience instead of a speculation. Words are here to model a bodily feeling of consciousness. It's ok to learn slow. After it becomes a bodily memory, you will be in a meditative awareness anytime you sit down cross-legged. It takes you through four stages of *clearing out thoughts*, *centering focus*, *panoramic presence*, and finally *dissolution of boundary*.

Now lets find a wall to sit in front of. A wall with texture is optimum. You will need to fix your eye sight onto a single point in part of the exercise. If not a texturized wall, an inked dot on a white wall will do just fine. Sit with legs crossed either on a yoga mat or a cushion not raised too high from the floor. Let's begin.

Stage 1:

Shift your awareness onto one simple, repetitive, rhythmic and sustaining event, such as counting beads or breathing.

Clear out thoughts. Be in the moment. Cut off any thoughts that distract your consciousness. Shift your awareness onto your breathing or counting beads. Feel your breath. Become your breath.

By clearing out thoughts, you become aware of the subtle inner being. It is an energetic field that is vibrant. Once you land in the subtle realm, conscious causality follows to be felt as you.

Notes:

- Some people count sheep to quiet the mind. But it's not an ideal subject to picture. Soon you will start to wonder what the sheep looks like, are they running or flying, etc. Instead, put awareness on your breathing or meditation beads without using the mind.

- Some teachings talk about allowing thoughts to come and go without attending to it. This approach is the essence of meditation. However, it is not the most practical training method. By allowing a thought to complete in time, you are already attending to its continuity. To let it go means that we need to cut off the tendency before it evolves into a finished thought.

Technique 1: Cutting Off Thought Before It Finishes

Thinking is a way of leaking energy. Another way to clear out thoughts is to actually feel as if you are dragging the energy back to your body from going outward.

Technique 2: Swinging Your Upper Body

In addition, you can also close your eyes and swing your upper body. This helps you to cut off thoughts and come back to the body.

The swing creates a sense of motion. When you are the consciousness that is manifesting through breathing, you're being the bodiless void within the motion of appearance.

This motion removes the gravitational certainty of sitting straight with fixed upside and downside. It frees you as a floating formless *perception* in the uncertain relationship with your body and gravity.

Swinging your upper body can help you feel your inner field. It subsides your awareness from gross-level objects to subtle-level beingness.

Lastly, be aware that the movement shouldn't be coming from for your body and mind's tendency to fidget.

Technique 3: Humming or Chanting

Humming a mono tone or chanting can also help calm your mind. Keep it low-pitch, because a low-pitch tone resonates your entire physical body, instead of just the top of the head. Chanting opens energy channels with vibration, similar to singing.

Vocal sound is a modulation of breath. Offering a chant is offering your breath, which is the interface between internal and external. Often times, your deep gentle breath will express as humming sound naturally.

Singing can be a good meditative experience on its own, especially singing improvisational harmony. It activates energy channels as well as brings out your causality.

During meditation, it can be good if your humming is manifested into some singing, but don't sing deliberately, because it can't also become an mind's distractive effort.

Technique 4: Closing Your Eyes

Shutting down your eyes gently can help you feel your inner field. Combined with the slow swinging of body and full breath, a inward awareness can shift attention from external shapes to internal realm of energy. This technique is helpful as a reset back to the subtle and causal realm. I have seen meditation masters use this technique combined with deep breath and elongation of spine to come back to absolute silent presence from casual laughter on group humor within a few seconds.

Remember not to shut your eyes for too long. It's easy to lose alertness and fall asleep. Moving to the next stage, open your eyes.

Stage 2:

Allow consciousness to reside in you. Be in your body. Gather consciousness into a thin line vertically through the body.

Your mind is constantly wandering around. And now we are going to drag that thought energy back to the center. This step is to focus your consciousness into a solid thin line. This line is vertically fixed from your head to your spine and down to the tailbone. Guard this centerline from moving or leaning. It's rock-solid protected and condensed through your upper body. All your consciousness is retracted onto this single line. You cut all your thoughts that distract or diffuse.

Now lock you eyes onto a single focal point. Try to project your state of being onto this point. Do not throw away consciousness towards it, but rather project along your sight from the un-moved centerline of consciousness. The state is experienced as if there's a horizontal pole between your centerline and the focal point, you acknowledge the object, but do not lean towards it. Your centerline feels being pushed backwards because the counter force from this pole. You pay attention to this single point as if all other objects around it disappear. Just your consciousness fixed inside of your body, and the chosen object perceived as one point. You look into the point and notice the inherent being this object exists as underneath its shape. The gazing is so strong that you see through form into its essence, the same essence of your subtle being.

Technique 4: Borrowing Essence from Space
This stage is the gaining of essence, allowing consciousness to embody as your spine. Your level of essence increases as the

air-like consciousness gathers inside your body into a solid thin line. You literally feel the rather pleasurable discomfort from rapid increase of essence. Your pelvic floor should sealed spontaneously when you feel the essence gain. The pelvis area is where energetic essence usually leaks out. In this feeling of essence gain, feel your pelvic floor sealed.

You absorb essence into your body from your surrounding space. Space is consciousness, and you are centering this consciousness into a solid line.

"I am in my body, looking at you. My mind is empty, my attention is full."

This is the emotional tone towards the point that you choose to fix sight upon.

Looking at one single object is to train yourself to "shoot out" from your centered consciousness. Project light from your center, not throwing away the light bulb.

The feeling is that you are creating a double of your state of being in that object, in a teleportational way. The feeling is also that *"I. am. in. you"*.

Technique 5: Pushing Hands
If you are meditating in front of a wall, you can hang you hands relaxedly in front of the center of your body in contact with the wall, and then add force towards it from your center structure. Almost like you are pushing the wall away while it's drawn

to come closer merging with you. The feeling is that you are already merged with the wall, yet your hands are pushing it away to maintain the tension of coming together. At the same time, through the contact of pushing hands you are physically connected with it.

Similar exercises are the essential trainings for many forms of martial arts such as Tai Chi and Wing Chun. In Wing Chun principles, Small Thoughts and Centerline are the core principles. Small thoughts means to cut out all necessities to attend, attacking on a single point with clarity. In meditation we project our undivided attention onto one point, in the space of awareness. In such meditative exercise, the essential feeling is also Small Thoughts and Centerline. Small thoughts onto the object, and centerline within yourself.

To project yourself onto anything, you have to have the tendency to come into it, as well as the distance in between. Strong intention of projection, and a virtualized pole or actual pushing hands in between you and the wall, these two techniques keep you steady and certain.

In this stage of meditation, the only existence is your consciousness and the point that you lock eyes onto. Nothing else, not even your body that exists.

Stage 3:
Relax your consciousness to fill your body. Comprehend the place. Become aware outwards. Your consciousness becomes

dyed air or fluid filling up your body. It often comes to me as purple smoke but might be felt as various other qualities. Your body becomes a chamber shaped by skin. Your skin crystallizes into a thin shell of a polished pottery. Inside this chamber is empty white space. The air of consciousness fills this chamber, becoming the shape of your body. And now every cubic inch inside your body is fogged with consciousness, your skin contains this consciousness into the shape of you.

Your eyes are still on the object, but your intention is retrieved back into your body, rather than being projected onto the object. As consciousness becomes the shape of your body, your eyes tend to open wide, perceiving everything in your sight as a whole. You perceive the environment as if it is a single focal point.

Your centerline of consciousness doesn't dissolve. Rather, more fluid consciousness appears in your body. This time, consciousness is in form of air instead of solid thin line. The air, filling up your body, becomes the shape of you. Your visual attention lays on the entire sight of vision, rather than isolating a single point.

At this stage, you maintain the centerline of consciousness solid and unwavering, but also feel more consciousness coming in to fill up your body in form of air. Your sight pays attention on the entire sight as if the whole picture is a single point, but also remain the ability of isolating one object to be your point of focus.

Your long and deep breath is pumping this air into your body.

Consciousness is filling you like a drop of ink diffusing into a bottle of water. Released from head into the whole body, each drop is making the color fuller.

The increasing-density consciousness is so full that it's pushing the shell of your skin outwards.

You are still focused. But your focus expands to everything in sight. As attention keeps expanding, you are feeling everything.

Stage 4:

Switch between stage two and three. Stage three makes you full and present, while stage two is about penetrating *through*. You are relaxed and open, full and present, yet alert and ready.

Stage two is to reduce everything into singularity. To know this singularity for absolute, and therefore realize the one-ness of consciousness through this singular point. When your attention focuses through one singular point, your attention is freed as infinity.

Stage three is to expand focus. Your attention has been freed in stages two by seeing through singularity and knowing for absolute. That freedom of attention is the same freedom when you expand your attention to feel everything. Stage three is to maintain that freedom of attention gained by reducing all possibility into one knowing for sure, and meanwhile using that freedom to feel everything. It is to use the freedom gained by focusing through a singularity, to feel everything.

The freedom got by feeling everything and feeling through one thing for absolute, is the same freedom as spacious consciousness.

Stage 5:
The paper-thin boundary of pottery chamber starts to dissolve. Consciousness is released outward. You no longer have a body. Your consciousness is one with the conscious light of everything, all light and sound. It's a whole conscious luminosity that knows itself, and therefore knows everything.

58.

Meditation Integration

Meditative sessions bring you back to the fundamental awareness. It is a great way to start a day,
or to practice whenever you feel distracted by
life's situations. This thoughtless panoramic awareness is
the ground for good Yoga practice. If you have a routine for
internal energy training, right after meditation makes the
perfect sequence. In between meditation and physical Hatha
Yoga, you can even add vocal warm-up, chanting or Chakra
Meditation – which is an internal yoga done without physical
movements. It's optimum to follow this meditation training
with Yoga, Qigong or Tai Chi Practice, or any internal energetic exercise. You will find that physical movements become

spontaneous and self-inventive. If you are going to climb or Parkour, also remember to stretch.

This is a series of practice on consciousness. Because it's a deliberate stretch between focus and relaxation, your mouth and jaw may tense up slightly at some point. It's normal in those condensed exercises. You can release the tension in lips and jaw by putting attention on the weight of the entire length of lower jaw, as well as by shifting awareness backwards onto the spine. You may even rotate the head forward to elongate upper part of spine that is in the back of neck.

Remember, the correction of muscular tension is in the realm of yoga, not meditation. You can be absolutely conscious even with a tense jaw. In fact, when you are absolutely present, you won't care if there's tension in the neck. It's not necessarily healthy depends on the extremity of your practice. Therefore yoga often comes in as a complement.

Meditation prescribed in the previous chapter is an exercise for the body to feel consciousness. You should disregard concerns of posture and breathing. Any attempt to correct posture and breathing will interrupt meditation. Of course, your breathing naturally becomes gentle and long. But it is a natural formation rather than a deliberate posing. After meditation, you can train body and breathing in Yoga.

In the end, meditation is a spontaneous discovery. It is an experiment that leads itself. You won't know how different it's going to feel next time. In deed, every meditation session is a different experience. Every experience, successful or less profound, is a piece of art on its own. To be consciousness necessitates you to see every situation as a piece of art, and puts you in a position that's in relationship with this art.

Even though the above exercise guides you one paragraph by another. Meditation is always an unprescribed feeling combined with the certainty of discipline, effortless-ness, and letting-it-go. Any effort added is a hindrance. These guided trainings are to be done over and over again, and to be let go of completely throughout the day.

59.

Workout as Meditation

Be the witness of pain. And do what you need to do. Working out is a great way to separate your consciousness from bodily sensation. It strips down your sense of self image, channeling the energy of purposeless thinking into a clear determination. It's a good exercise for identifying consciousness in uncomfortable situations. It trains the necessary decisiveness for self discipline.

On the one hand, the muscular activity makes you feel your body's energetic field. You have to access consciousness to push through physical stress, determining to keep working regardless of the discomfort. This separates your external recognition from the conscious self.

The masculine approach to openness is through narrowing all possibilities into one single focal point, and then going through this singularity to all possibilities. The Masculine recognizes the openness of infinity by drilling through one single point of focus.

Going to the gym is to push yourself. Everything in your head is put aside because you need that total focus to push, even though your muscles are under stress. To override sensation is to condense the embodiment of consciousness. You have to identify with consciousness so much that all thoughts are emptied out. You breathe full into your belly, you lightly close your eyes, all you see is the singularity of a goal.

In this intense focus, you go through the single focal point into a vast awareness, which is also consciousness and love.

This is the proper training of masculinity, not by resisting, but by feeling through appearance.

60

Meditation with Candle

_Training on Presence, Polarity and Sensitivity

A flame has the most flexible body. It is literally light and energy. A flame can be calm and healing, or chaotic and violent. Either way, it is energy and light.

A flame needs your nourishment and protection. You have to develop sensibility to feel her. But be careful because it can also burn you. Even the smallest flame can kill you, if you are not present with her with sensitivity. If you are distracted.

Meditating with candle, you are also watching nature's formation. She is consuming the candle, and discharging the burnt.

A flame has a form of warmth. Warmth is a part of her. You can feel her with you skin. Feel her with your body. In the snow, this warmth is what saves your life. Feel through this warmth, as the space that manifests this warmth is what manifests all appearance.

When meditating in front of a candle, she is the brightest light source in the room, literally. It's just you and her. She has your full attention. You are feeling her continuously.

She represents energy that is sometimes calm and sometimes chaotic. Yet you remain still, not grasping on her disturbance. You are allowing her to be gentle or violent, as the space where she appears.

A flame indicates air movement. By feeling the dance of a flame, you are feeling the liquidity that is surrounding all of us right now.

A flame will die, just as every moment will be gone. Let go of the companionship in the end. Be sitting there in your body with contentment. That is abundant with ease. You need nothing other than nothing itself. Next time you light up a candle, it will be a different flame. Yet it is also the same flame. The love that appears as her light, her energy and her warmth is still the one, which can never be apart from you. What manifests a flame is what manifests your form and all appearing forms. It is your light. You are the space that allows it to happen. You and this light are never apart.

A flame is a girl. She comes to this world and you are the only person she will ever see. You are all that she has. So be with her completely, from her birth, to her flourish, till her death. Be with her. Feel her through and through. Protect her with sensitivity, until her last breath.

Because the light source is different than that of what we are accustomed to, we perceive objects as new in candle light.

The color of wall is different. The yellow casted on the ceiling is brightening and dimming. The environment is shifted into a new reality for you.

The next practice is to face a wall to meditate in candle light. The wall doesn't move but the light shimmers. The reality of room literally fluctuates with candle light. In any moment, the world as you know it could be gone. As a candle lights up existence, it's bright and calm at times and yet can be threatened by the wind. All of the flux cannot waver wall's certainty. That is the certainty you need to be.

When you die, don't look left, don't look right. Look straight ahead. Otherwise you will be sucked back to this place again.

In this case, the candle light becomes the appearance. It is the light as well as the distraction. Can you see through it to the wall that doesn't change. Can you stay with the wall while the lighting fluctuates. Can you feel the movement of the candle light while maintaining sight of what's always there.

Chapter 15:
Ending

61.

Giving Love
is the Only Salvation

Pack the happiness you have had, and give it away
as a gift. Harboring any past is the source of tension.
Give it to people in pain, leaving not even a memory.

Soon enough, this moment will be your last.

We have limited ability to transmute emotions. Neutral enough, pain and pleasure are both a part of life. There are only much you can do about it.

However, we can choose to not let waste of our pain and suffer. Only by giving love to the world tirelessly until it kills us can we find our salvation.

All lives are ultimately meaningless. The choice is yours, to give love or to hold back. You could have been in the afterlife, dead already. With what's left in you, go create openness.

Make gold from your suffering, so the world suffer less. Give away your happiness, so memory won't bind you.

Do what you can to give love, with the spirit in your creation, with whatever shit you have left.

It isn't about us. A good life ends in a noble death. Meaning can not be found in gain or loss. Everything will be broken and then forgotten. We do not have anything. As there is nothing to lose, endings will not take away anything.